Transcend!

Quo Vadis Negotiator

Pompeii, Italy. Picture: Habib Chamoun-Farah

Pillars of Transcendental Negotiation

Dr. Habib Chamoun-Nicolás

In collaboration with

Enrique Martin Baena

Dr. Randy D. Hazlett

Hernan Pereda Bullrich

All Rights Reserved, Copyright ©2018
Keynegotiations
Book *Transcend! Quo Vadis Negotiator*
Library of Congress Control Number
LCCN: 2016917583
ISBN- 978-0-9728317-5-8

Printed in the United States of America Special Edition, First Edition ©2016 Dr. Habib Chamoun-Nicolás

English Translation©2018 Dr. Habib Chamoun-Nicolás

No part of this publication may be reproduced, stored in a retrieval system or transmitted in any form or by any means electronic, mechanical, photocopying, recording or otherwise, without the prior written permission of Dr. Habib Chamoun-Nicolás.

Limit of Liability / Disclaimer of Warranty: While the publisher and the author have used their best efforts in preparing this book, they make no representations or warranties with respect to the accuracy or completeness of the contents of this book and specifically disclaim any implied warranties of merchantability or fitness for a particular purpose. No warranty may be created or extended by sales representatives of written sales materials. The advice and strategies contained herein may not be suitable for your situation. You should consult a professional when appropriate. Neither the publisher nor the author shall be liable for any loss of profit or any other commercial damages, included but not limited to special, incidental, consequential or other damages.

All references concerning Scriptures, unless otherwise stated, have been taken from the New International Version of the Holy Bible. Copyright 1973, 1978, 1984 of the International Bible Society. Permission authorized by Zondervan. All rights reserved. Cover design by Claudette Farah Chalita and Randy Hazlett. All Rights Reserved. All photos were taken by Habib Chamoun-Nicolás, with the exception of those stated otherwise.

Front cover by artist Claudette Farah Chalita, www.claudettefarah.com
Everyone has a mountain to climb in life full of obstacles ... Live! and Transcend!

Acknowledgments

First of all, I would like to thank God for giving us the gift to express in this work how to "Transcend" the negotiation. This work would not be possible without the unconditional support of my better half, my wife Marcela, and my four children. For your patience and consideration, thank you, Habib, Emile, Antoine and Marcelle.

Second, I would like to thank my colleagues for their gift of patience and dedication in arduous and specific work done by the Madrid, Houston and Tulsa teams. It is noteworthy that we all come from different contexts and academic disciplines and physically we are in different geographical locations.

Third, I appreciate the confidence and wisdom of two people who I not only admire, but that I am fortunate to have as part of my family. On the one hand, thanks to Enrique Martin Baena, who has brilliantly managed to interrelate concepts of the philosophical and anthropological world with concepts from the field of business. Some of the material presented in this book comes from his thesis titled "Neumatologia and spiritual discernment Ignaciano, Madrid 2001". On the other hand, thanks to Hernan Pereda Bullrich, a great communicator and historian, for the contribution of concepts of transcendence in his work *The Sense of History*.

I also take this opportunity to express my gratitude to my friend, colleague and collaborator of many years, Dr.

Randy Hazlett, for his valuable scientific and academic cooperation. In addition, advocating for the quality of the data presented in this work, I deeply appreciate the participation in the Spanish Edition from Elena Moreno Ugena of Madrid, for ensuring the quality of the writing. To my dear editor in Mexico City, Luza Alvarado, for ensuring the final details and making the content of this book engaging in one beautiful piece. Special thanks for reviewing the English edition to Marvin Brandon and Nick Ewing.

I am grateful and honored to have the book's Foreword written by Harvard Business School Senior Fellow and Professor Dr. Michael Wheeler and the Introduction by Max M. Fisher College of Business Professor Dr. Roy Lewicki, two of my great academic mentors and friends.

To Dr. Larry Susskind for his great comments on this work and for his guidance and friendship.

Thank you with appreciation and admiration to a woman role model leader with ethics, principles and fundamental values based in the family union. I am honored by her prologue to this book in the Spanish edition that is a worthy contemporary example of someone who transcends, my friend Josefina Vazquez Mota, a person who has left her mark as the first female candidate for the Presidency of the Mexican Republic by a majority party.

To my dear Professor David Noel Ramirez, former Dean of Monterrey TEC in Mexico for his emotional introduction to this book in the Spanish edition.

To Clau Farah Chalita, to "live" transcendence in her work.

To my brothers and sister, Yamal, Anuar and Soraya. Thanks.

To my friend Alfonso Daumas and family for sharing their stories.

To the academic collaborators in Guatemala, especially to Ana Izabel de Matta Vega, from Universidad del Istmo, with whom I had worked an investigation of intercultural and intracultural negotiation, part of which appears in this book.

To all my friends from Cadiz, especially to Dr. Manolo Calero; and the archaeologists José María Gener and Ana Niveau; to our Atheneist friends of Cadiz, Don Enrique Garcia Agullo and Francisco Glicerio Conde Mora. To my friend, Dr. Christian Joksch, for his support filming the project Cadiz-Puerto Vallarta.

To my colleagues James Chiu, José Antonio Hernández Ruiz, Victoria Alejandra Valdés, Sandra Maycotte Felkel, Dr. Francisco Valderrey, Pedro Carreón Gutiérrez, Walid Sabaj, Dr. Genaro Gutiérrez, Giovanni Rolando Solís and Arturo Oliver. To my dear friend and colleague Antonio Sánchez Diaz de Rivera, from the UPAEP in Puebla, and my dear Dr. Guillermo Cantú, professor and researcher from the PanAmerican University in Mexico City. To the revered Frank Donio and Armando Regil. To my dear Audrey R. Tetteh, ICONS project director from the University of Maryland. To the Cistercian monks from the Monastery of the Holy Cross in Austria, and especially to Dr. Karl

Josef Wallner, professor and rector of the Philosophisch-Theologische Hochschule Benedikt XVI, Heiligenkreuz.

Also thanks to all the media who have contributed with information, such as the *Journal of Cadiz, Andalusia World and Vallarta Opina*. Special thanks to Don Luis Reyes Brambila and Miguel Ángel Ocaña Reyes.

To my colleagues from the project Rethinking Negotiation Teaching, thanks for authorizing the use of part of our research published by you. Special thanks to Christopher Honeyman, James Coben, Giuseppe De Palo, Kenneth H. Fox, Andrea Schneider, and Melissa Manwaring.

To my Novancia Business School of Paris colleagues, to Dr. Doudou Sidibe and Emmanuelle Khvatov; to Dr. Angel Algarra, Sergio Cardona Patau, Alejandra Villena and Carmen Fernández, from CEU San Pablo, in Madrid; to Dr. Carlos G. Wagner, president of the Center for Studies Phoenician and Punic at the Complutense University of Madrid (CEFYP), for their support on the academic trip "Exploring the Phoenician Route", referred to here as a story. Special thanks to Dr. Carlos G. Wagner for his contributions of Phoenician anecdotes mentioned in this book; also, thanks to Salim Khalaf and Dr. Nick Kahwaji. Thanks to my dear friend Ambassador Massoud Maalouf for his valuable comments on this book.

To "los Cooperadores Parroquiales de Cristo Rey (CPCR)" all around the globe and especially in Madrid and Argentina: to Philippe Barbier, Hugo Massimino, Francisco Domínguez, Rafael García and Brothers.

To the Cameron School of Business at the Universidad

of St. Thomas in Houston; to IMADEC University, McCombs School of Business UT Austin; Texas A&M Kingsville; to the Istmo University, Monterrey TEC – Saltillo, Querétaro, León, Irapuato, and Torreón campuses– to the UPAEP, Novancia Business School of Paris; and the CEU San Pablo, in Madrid.

To my dear colleagues and professors from different business schools around the globe, especially to Dr. Natalya Delcoure, Dr. Beena George, Dr. Bahman Mirshab, Dr. Shahram Taj, Dra. Vinita Ramaswamy, Dra. Sidika Gespec Bayram, Dra. Sujin Horwitz, Dra. Elham Mousavidin, Dr. Charlene Dickman, Dr. Hassan Shirvani.

Thanks to all for your valuable comments on the book. If I had to name the people that have contributed directly or indirectly to put this book together I would need to write another book. I have the fortune and gratitude to have met so many people in my life that have given me something without even noticing. Thanks to you all. Thanks to my students, clients, colleagues, friends and family.

Habib Chamoun-Nicolás

Table of Contents

FOREWORD xvi

INTRODUCTION xx

CHAPTER I. NEGOTIATE WITH FAITH 1
Motivation 2
Negotiator Dilemma 8
From Silence to Fullness 12
Darkness as an Opportunity 19
Transgenerational Negotiation 23
"I am Sorry, I am Greek" 26
Creating a Desert 32
Be to Transcend 36
Negotiating with Meaning 41
Phoenician Heritage 47
Bartering, a Current Tool 56

CHAPTER II. PRUDENCE 69
What Do We Mean by Prudence? 70
Collaborative Negotiation 72
Tradeables and Prudence in Negotiation 80
The Philosophy of Giving 83
What Are the Needs of My Client? 86
Tradeables Categorization 93
Exercise Prudence 97
Ask Before You React 102
Prudence and Imprudence 107
Reflection Exercise 115

CHAPTER III. JUSTICE 117
What Do We Understand by Justice? 118
Injustice 123
Justice On a Large Scale 126
Reflection Exercise 137

CHAPTER IV. FORTITUDE 139
To Understand Fortitude 140
Turning Vulnerability into Fortitude 143
Against Anger and Fear 152
Gratitude, Gratuitousness and Fortitude 161
Psychic Strength 168
Reflection Exercise 176

CHAPTER V. TEMPERANCE 177
What is Temperance? 178
Two Eternal Loves 184

CHAPTER VI. DISCERNMENT 199
Choose by Way of Discernment 200
Decisive Stages in Negotiation 208
The Need for Discernment 211
Daily Thermometer of Negotiation 220
The Foundation of Indifference 222
14 Rules to Negotiate with Faith 224
Self-fulfilling Prophecy 248
Case Study: The Journey of Wenamen 251
Chapters Summary 260

GENERAL CONCLUSION 265

WHAT THE EXPERTS ARE SAYING 267

BIBLIOGRAPHY.. 276

FOREWORD

In this ground-breaking and inspiring book, Dr. Habib Chamoun-Nicolas generously explains how the key to dealing with others successfully requires first looking inward.

That's because whenever you negotiate with self, you implicitly define yourself. All that you do and say reflects aspects of your nature, your personality, and your character. Those actions comprise who you truly are, especially who you are in relation to others. *Transcend!* illuminates that reality and brings into focus two complementary insights that are essential for negotiators. One of them may seem obvious. The other is less so, though no less important.

The first is that negotiation is a profoundly human activity, one that can bring out the best in us, but only if we recognize the full consequences of the choices that we make. When we're not self-aware, we risk behaving in ways that conflict with our ideals.

Transactions of any sort raise moral issues about what we owe—if anything—in terms of fairness to the parties with whom we deal. Issues of fairness come up in different forms. One is honesty. For example, is it ever permissible to lie in negotiation? Many people would say never (or very rarely), though we may wonder whether they themselves truly live up to that principle. People start to squirm if asked whether nondisclosure—withholding key facts without lying overtly—is any better, given that the intent to mislead is no different. In practice, negotiators seem to apply a double standard by being comfortable with their own evasions, yet angry when others are less than fully candid.

Tactical choices in the course of negotiation raise moral issues, as well. Is it okay to bluff or use false deadlines to force concessions? "Certainly," some people might claim. "It's a game like poker. Everyone understands the rules." Yes, sharp bargainers may prevail in some circumstances, but that attitude imposes a social cost. It casts negotiation as a contest, with a winner and loser. The participants themselves are foes, not potential partners. That competitive view isn't universal, of course, but it makes people who do not subscribe to it approach the table with some caution, lest they be manipulated. As a result, they may hesitate to trust others and reveal their true priorities. When that happens, opportunities for value-creating solutions can be squandered.

That leads us to the third level of moral issues, the fairness of the ultimate outcome—who gets what share of the pie. The question does not have an easy answer. Much depends on circumstances. Perhaps a customer shopping for a new car need not worry about how the dealership makes out. Even if she is well-prepared, the salesman will know more about the market and his and/or the dealership's needs than she ever will. If she makes an unreasonable offer, the salesperson can always say no. But imagine that those parties reach agreement, and it is now nine years later. She's considering selling the well-used vehicle to a teenager for whom it will be his first car. Many would argue that she should think twice about squeezing him out of every last dollar that he's earned in his after-school job.

At the outset, I stated that the moral dimension of negotiation is obvious. That may be true in the abstract, but in actual practice, the pressures of the process (including balancing competing responsibilities to oneself and to others) can narrow our vision and undermine our ability to live up to our professed values.

It is on this plane that *Transcend!* makes a unique contribution to negotiation wisdom. Its conceptual framework links together important skills that not only can enable a negotiator to maintain perspective, but can also enhance his or her substantive performance. Among these are *prudence, fortitude, temperance,* and *discernment.* I'm tempted to call those attributes "virtues," as they are most certainly aspects of character. I have stayed with "skills," however, to make clear the practicality of this work. Each of the skills is explained with concrete examples, and there are reflective exercises, as well. The point is that we can all deepen these qualities, through practice and attention.

The book you are holding provides numerous compelling explanations and applications. Here are two examples: First, Chapter 5 describes temperance as "the act of creating order in our own self as a kind of self-preservation, a habit that defends and protects us from ourselves, due to the fact that humans have a strong tendency of going against one's own nature." In short, we need poise and balance to perform at our best.

Renowned mediator David Hoffman speaks of the importance of "bringing peace into the room" when he handles other people's disputes. As this book makes clear, negotiators likewise must strive for the same kind of balance. Emotions are contagious. If we are tense and internally conflicted, others will sense it and respond accordingly.

The nature of interpersonal dynamics is developed further in the concluding chapter on discernment (an important word that I can't recall seeing in any other negotiation text). A section warns of the danger of self-fulfilling prophecies that occur when "whatever we infer about a person becomes a reality, not because the inference is correct, but because our fearful or defensive action produces a similar reaction in the other. The inference causes us, rather than dealing with a person, to deal with a ghost that we have created of that person."

Amen to that.

In hindsight, it's sometimes possible to recognize how others may have misread our defensiveness as hostility and how we may have projected our own feelings on them. But then, it's too late. The challenge—indeed, the imperative—is anticipating that possibility and engaging others in an open and constructive manner. By summoning the best in ourselves, we can endeavor to evoke the best in others with whom we deal.

Michael Wheeler
Harvard Business School

INTRODUCTION

The world of negotiation books—for both students and practitioners—can largely be grouped into several categories.

First, there are numerous books that report on the works and practices of *great negotiators* (Stanton, 2011) offering biographical perspectives on these individuals and highlighting their conduct in significant negotiation events. Many of these works are in the fields of political science and international relations, where it is more 'professionally acceptable' to perform scholarly work by reporting information about the substance, structure and evolution of complex deals, such as boundary disputes, peace-building and peacekeeping efforts, tribal conflicts, and resolution of major economic, political and social conflict. In reading these, one learns a great deal about the complexity of the dispute, while also gaining insight into the talents and skills of the key negotiators.

Second, one can find more academic 'textbooks' on negotiation, which blend an extensive body of research together into a summary of the 'science' of negotiation (e.g., Lewicki, Saunders and Barry, 2015; Thompson, 2014) . These books integrate the findings from many scientifically designed and controlled studies, each studying one or two key variables (e.g., differences in personality type, tactic use and effectiveness, context in which the negotiation occurs), into a synthetic whole that provides multiple lenses and perspectives on the complex interpersonal and group dynamics of a negotiation. While these books are largely descriptive in their presentation of the research findings, they are also mildly prescriptive—but quite antiseptic—in offering their advice about how to use the research to improve one's negotiation practice.

Finally, the vast majority of books on negotiation are written for the practicing negotiator, and offer 'distilled' wisdom about how to understand the give and take of a negotiation and how to master this give and take. A few of these books offer their prescriptive advice by grounding it in the solid findings of the research tradition, but most offer helpful tips, techniques and tools that a negotiator can use in order to 'win' (e.g., Fisher, Ury and Patton, 2013; Latz, 2004). These books usually reflect the professional background of the author (e.g., real estate, purchasing, law, business transactions) and are replete with examples, vignettes, war stories and other applications designed to make the key points. While many have high value for the practicing negotiator, few offer a truly comprehensive perspective on the complex dynamics of parties working to find an acceptable solution to a nagging, complex and pervasive dispute.

Remarkably, *Transcend! Quo Vadis Negotiator* does not conveniently fit any of these categories. Rather, Habib Chamoun and his collaborators offer us the opportunity to take a personal journey into ourselves as negotiators. The authors' perspective is that we must know ourselves as human beings—more than just our strengths and weaknesses, but also our *character*—before we can seriously engage in the planning, strategy and tactical execution of a complex deal. The proper lenses for this self-knowledge are the organizing theme of this book and, as Dean David Noel Ramirez notes in his introduction to the Spanish version, are 'precepts that have existed since ancient times': Prudence, Justice, Fortitude, Temperance and Discernment.

This book makes three major contributions that offer significant enrichment to both the budding negotiator and the highly experienced dealmaker. First, it does not try to follow the typical 'know thyself' road of many similar books by dealing with the simple 'paper and pencil' self-assessments typically used in negotiating seminars and courses, such as indicators of conflict management style, leadership or communication style, or basic fundamental dimensions of personality. Instead it encourages the reader to delve deeply into his or her personal *values,* since these values are likely to be the strongest determinant of the fundamental mindset and personal biases that an individual brings to the negotiation table. Second, it is usefully prescriptive in that it outlines the five basic values (virtues) that must govern a productive, mutual gains negotiation, and implicitly creates the tools for negotiators to assess where they personally stand on those values. Finally, by addressing negotiation character directly, the authors are also able to offer advice on how to begin to reason through value dilemmas, particularly ones involving the use of dishonest and deceptive tactics. As any experienced negotiator knows, these are the tactics which may help one gain short-term advantage but also can create irreparable damage to any long-term relationship with a strategic partner. As such, *Transcend!* offers a most valuable and unique contribution to the negotiation literature, one that should be required reading for all who expect to spend a life and career in ongoing negotiation and dispute resolution.

Roy J. Lewicki
Max M. Fisher College of Business, The Ohio State University

CHAPTER I

NEGOTIATE WITH FAITH

To negotiate with faith is not the same as having faith in the negotiation. Cistercian Monastery of the Holy Cross, Austria

MOTIVATION

There is extensive literature on the subject of negotiation; however, we found few texts that directly address the theme of training negotiators in ethical principles and common sense (Menkel-Meadow & Wheeler, 2004), and even rarer are works that examine man as a negotiator from the anthropological point of view. It is this lack of literature that motivated us to write this book, which requires joining the old with the new, the technocratic with the humanist, and leads to the formation of a negotiator's comprehensive vision.

This book is aimed toward all people, to formulate an analysis of consciousness upon an anthropological foundation for negotiation. This is not to avoid the mere interchange of goods, but to include in this activity a more transcendental vision.

Negotiation is not only an instrument of purpose, it is a purposeful outcome, because there's something in me that is growing, putting my whole being at stake. We will define negotiation in this book not only as the typical act of haggling or distributive bargaining, the give and take, but also as the creative environment to generate options, such as integrative bargaining and, above all, the search for permanence and significance for future generations (transgenerational tradeables).

Negotiation is a continuous dance of postures. Through a process of communication and persuasion, you can discover the interests behind the postures, which finally help generate options to meet the interests of the parties and reach an agreement, or, failing that, to seek the best alternative.

If we approach negotiating more as an art, the negotiator is more likely to move from the transaction to the transcendent. What is transcendence in the negotiation?

When we only focus on the transaction of simple objects or services, we will not necessarily leave a mark on future generations, as we are only focused on doing and having in the present.

Grandparents used to proactively advocate dealing with others on ethical foundations. The family name was worth more than money. Tarnish to the family name could not be compensated, because the damage extended several generations. Not long ago, the last name of the person was all you needed to give credibility and trust. Moreover, if one asked for a bank loan, the family name reputation was sufficient collateral.

If Grandpa had a reliable and reputable business, this provided leverage when the grandson negotiated, as long as the grandson continued with the same philosophy, building upon his grandfather's legacy. To transcend in business is to create the best conditions in the present and consolidate them for future generations. To achieve this, we must concentrate on what we are; we must focus on Being.

Our surroundings echo signs of significance in the history of mankind. This rock contains Roman inscriptions of Emperor Marcus Aurelius (178-179 AD) at the Castle of Tencin, Slovakia, anchoring both old and new foundations.

One reason many family businesses fail in the second generation is that the sons and daughters do not bother to transcend. In the next negotiation in which you participate, ask yourself if you'll leave a positive, permanent mark.

Will I show my children how to be an ethical negotiator? Are my children going to feel ashamed of my negotiations, because my example only focused on getting as much as I can?

Transcending the negotiation requires that the negotiator is able to keep his word, as did his ancestors. A responsibility fulfilled transcends to past and future generations. However, new generations do not have clarity in their identity; today's culture tends to homogenize and to dismiss the value of family ownership. In this context, forming ethical negotiators involves a series of principles that are the basis of our civilization. These pillars are prudence, justice, fortitude, temperance and discernment. In addition to analyzing these pillars in this work, we give some examples and anecdotes to reflect together on the transcendental sense of negotiation.

This transcendental dimension of negotiation also incorporates the notion of common good that, as suggested by Pope Francis I, involves considering future generations. International economic crises have starkly shown harmful effects brought about by a failure to recognize a common destiny, the fallout from which cannot exclude those who come after us. You cannot talk about sustainable development without intergenerational solidarity. When we think about the planet we leave to future generations and how we are educating them, we enter into another dynamic, the free gift we receive and communicate. While the earth is a gift, it does not belong to us; therefore, we cannot act from a utilitarian criterion of efficiency and productivity for individual benefit. We are not talking about an optional attitude but a basic question of justice, since the land we received also belongs to those who come after us.

While exploring these pillars in your reading, I recommend that you perform self-analysis with the tools provided and reflect upon your position as a negotiator with ethical sense. To assist you, at the end of each chapter you will find a series of questions for self-assessment to gauge your level of consciousness on each topic and measure your ability to transcend in the negotiations. (You will see this only applies to three pillars, as traditionally, discernment and prudence are interchangeable terms.) Finding the meaning of things is of great importance in all human activity, so we will be analyzing the Meaning of Negotiation throughout this work. Finally, in the reflection process, we will see how to integrate conflict management and how to harmonize intellectual abilities with the will and affections.

The large pillars that give meaning to the negotiation: prudence, justice, fortitude, temperance and discernment. Photo taken at the Cistercian Monastery of the Holy Cross in the Vienna Austria forests

NEGOTIATOR DILEMMA

When making decisions in the negotiation process, we can find that on the road to the agreement there are possible dilemmas and conflicts in decision-making that must be addressed that can build bridges or barriers, generate weaknesses or strengths, or result in emptiness or fullness.

Many know the story of Samson and Delilah. In the Hebrew scriptures, the book of Judges tells how Delilah manipulated Samson to tell her the secret of his supernatural strength. Following this revelation, he was imprisoned and eventually sentenced to death, dragging with him a considerable number of his foes. We've all been in a similar dilemma: do I tell or not tell you? Is he manipulating me? Is he telling the truth? The story of Samson illustrates that strength is insufficient when swept away by seduction. Discernment is essential to avoid making decisions that, as in the case of Samson, lead to dire consequences.

In a negotiation framework, a dilemma occurs when we cooperate and compete simultaneously. On the one hand, we want to communicate and try to understand each other's position to improve our position; we want to compete to achieve our greatest gain. Any action of competitive negotiation holds the objective, ultimately, to distribute the value. For example, if there are 100, and I am left with 80, the other will be left with 20. However, if the other begins to compete, this changes the distribution.

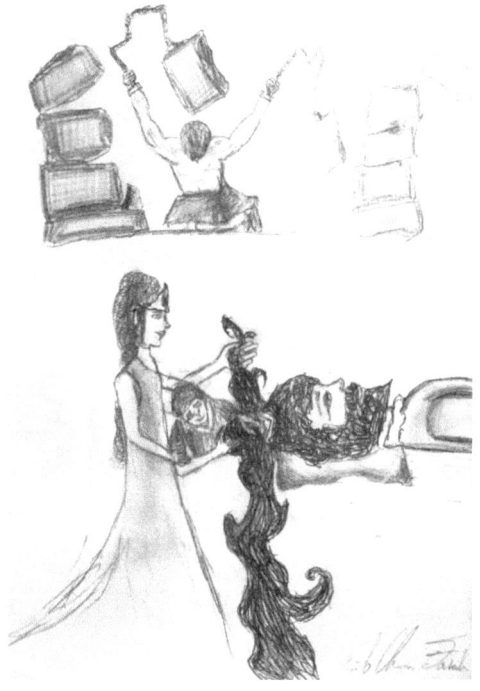

The fort is not as strong as it looks when it is carried away by seduction. Illustration: Samson and Delilah,
Emile Chamoun-Farah

We enter a tug of war, but we also see the need to work to not leave behind value on the negotiating table. The dilemma is summarized in a question:

Should I compete, or should I collaborate?

An equally valuable question:

Can this negotiation be integrative, or must we divide the value?

If the other wants to pay only 10, and I desire 20, we will be competing to reach a value to which both agree. That is, we will distribute the value that is on the table. This is called distributive or position-based negotiation, and it is the dynamic of haggling and bargaining. In this type of negotiation, there is a resistance price of the buyer and a resistance price of the seller. The difference between these two prices is called the zone of possible agreement. We must also be aware of the maximum and minimum prices that both sides are willing to pay. Beware of anchors that are generated with the first offer that becomes the reference position for each negotiator. Sometimes negotiators who are anchored in a position resist all movement.

Integrative negotiation seeks to foster relationship between the parties with communication to understand the motivation behind one another's posture. If I understand in depth the interests of both sides, I can generate options with legitimacy and references.

Another element to ponder is the commitment to disclosure. We may reach an agreement, but it is possible that we will not. Sometimes we must consider the best alternative to negotiated agreement (BATNA).

A classic example to understand the difference between distributive and integrative negotiation is the one given to us by Ury and Fisher, two experts from Harvard. A man has two oranges and two daughters. How should he divide the oranges? When I ask this question in my courses, people respond with a win-win solution to give an orange to each. That would be the distributive solution or position-based outcome. However, if the relationship and communication between the man and his daughters is open, he can probe to understand the interest of each of his daughters concerning the oranges. This is where integrative or interest-based negotiation comes in. When asked why each of them wants the orange, one of the daughters responds that she wants to make orange juice; therefore, she needs the pulp, while the other says she wants to make a cake, and thus only needs the orange peel. The negotiator (the father) enters a circle of value and can generate options, such as giving the pulp to one daughter and the skin to the other daughter. Thus, the initial value satisfies multiple stakeholders' needs completely. Everyone wins.

Throughout our reflections, we see the need to create "thoughts that overcome the fragility of the world," as the writer Gao Xingjian said. One way is to learn to distinguish the ordinary from the extraordinary, what is worthwhile and what is worthless.

FROM SILENCE TO FULLNESS

I was invited as a professor to spend a few days in the Cistercian monastery of the Holy Cross, in the woods of Austria. The experience was unforgettable and very deep. I arrived with a friend who left me during the church service. I discovered that the atmosphere of the monastery causes all noises to be blocked and enables one to hear the echo of one's own being. At the conclusion of the Gregorian chants, the monks simply pulled me into their ranks. I followed a line of monks in silence, as a military recruit unquestioningly follows instructions from his commanding officer. Order and silence was broken only by the sound of water trickling from a nearby fountain in the forbidden garden. I was at the core of the monastery where only monks live. To arrive at our living quarters, I had to pass by that forbidden garden, nestled in shadows.

The atmosphere of the monastery created an encounter with myself.

I felt I was walking through a labyrinth, accompanied by the echoing of an enchanted fountain and flanked by a maze of routes connecting the monastery with the church and the living quarters.

Order and silence were only broken by the sound of the water.

These were not ordinary monks; their voices were angelic when singing Gregorian chants. I spent seven days in November in the monastery, immersed in the daily life of a monk. Initially, living in the monastery was a spooky experience, but I reminded myself that I was blessed and privileged to have this unique opportunity in life, especially since the monks did not allow just anyone to share their daily life.

The monks' motto was *"Ora et Labora et Docet",* which translates to pray, work and teach. I suddenly felt connected by a very strong bond with the monks and the monastery. I strongly believe that a person can be seen as saintly through evidence of their work.

However, for these monks, that was not enough; you needed to pray, work and teach. I felt that my soul was connected to the monks, including my philosophy of life. I was honored as a guest professor for the day. For a layman, this was a once-in-a-lifetime moment. I entered a dining room crowded with beautiful frescos to a round of applause. I reflected on what life would have been like in 1200 A.D. I imagined it would have been very similar to what I was experiencing. Following prayer, we sat in our assigned places.

Everything was very formal. The monks would set their glass upright at the sound of a bell for drinks to be served, followed by their daily meal. The monks took turns serving one another. During lunch, they listened to the word of the Lord, and every minute was full of reflections, prayer and silence. What a treat for someone like me who is not used to such periods of absolute silence. Prayer was always followed by complete silence. There was a morning prayer and a last prayer of the night. The first day for me was most challenging and uncomfortable. However, as the week progressed, I found an internal peace never before experienced. By day seven, I was thankful for the opportunity to self-reflect in silence and peace.

Praying, Working, and Teaching help to reach internal peace and fullness

In fact, I strongly believe I encountered a person of the Trinity—the Holy Spirit. I was in such a peaceful mindset that I no longer felt scared when walking alone by the forbidden garden late at night or very early in the morning when no one was present. I walked throughout the monastery and felt completely safe and peaceful. In fact, this is similar to entering into a cross-cultural experience. "The more one engages in cross-cultural experiences, the more one gets to understand oneself" (Goh 1996).

I believe blocking all noise was the best moment I have ever experienced. I had an opportunity to hear my internal voices without distraction, provoking a context to become a better listener. Focusing efforts toward a given goal and objective is a must in any negotiation.

The experience of the monastery was of great help in becoming a better negotiator, since the first key to negotiation is active listening. Forced silence heightens the sense of hearing and connection to the environment. Similarly, internal listening helps us to understand the other in context. The silence of the monastery put everything in perspective. Just as there are ideas, thoughts, actions and behaviors that can overshadow the extraordinary, there are others who transform what seems ordinary. We are known by what we repeatedly do, so we can become ordinary or extraordinary beings, depending on our free choice. The key is to find the beauty even in the ordinary and make it extraordinary.

Experiences like this can help us find prosperity within the depths of our being. The maze of life can lead to an encounter with ourselves and cause us to question our daily actions and find a sense of belonging and identity. On the other hand, isolation and depravity can make us feel lost, to the point of falling into neglect and loneliness.

The dilemma of a negotiator is whether to be or not to be ethical, and it has to do with our ability to distinguish the ordinary from the extraordinary: what is worthwhile and what is worthless.

Hernan Pereda Bullrich said that the value of a person is not based in what he has, or even on what he does, but rather on what he is, because "Having" and "Doing" depend on "Self." Knowing our value gives us confidence in what we do; we give the right weight to what we have. This makes us strong and helps us not to fall into the game of seduction.

The Phoenicians, an ancient civilization, were proud of themselves. They did not need to go to war to assert their value and identity, except when they were invaded. The Phoenicians transcended nearly 4000 years ago as the best negotiators in the world, and even today are remembered as such. Postmodern man, however, is in a maze of insecurities, and he does not know where he is going or from where he is coming. If he wants to find the exit, he has to connect with himself and find meaning. He has to listen to the most immediate and direct intuitive intelligence. We must start by creating a context to become a better listener and build an optimal condition to focus our efforts toward a goal.

The experience I had at the monastery helped me find prosperity within the depths of my being.

Transcendance in the negotiation teaches us about giving rather than getting. One of the possible results of a negotiation is prosperity. This should not be achieved at the expense of others, however, but with others, giving each one what is needed. Prosperity is reached when one is in harmony with oneself and with others, i.e., when there is inner peace. If at the end of the road we do not feel satisfied, although the negotiations have been successful, chances are we've lost focus on the way. Let's go back and ask ourselves: what I am negotiating? Deep down, what moves us to negotiate is the desire to meet the needs of others for ourselves to achieve the fullness of "Being". In a negotiation, this occurs when both sides give something meaningful to each other.

Fullness need not be confused with the pursuit of happiness. The latter is the result of an individual passion for living life. Fullness, however, comes when the encounter with others helps us discover our value and gives us a sense of belonging. We are confident that everything is in place, every evening and sunset, every detail. Every moment is measured by the feeling of being and belonging.

DARKNESS AS AN OPPORTUNITY

The last day before leaving the monastery, I was prepared to start a new journey full of listening skills, hope and light. I believed this was the most challenging experience I would encounter in life until I visited Hong Kong. There, I experienced the most "unusual" dinner with colleagues from around the globe.

Dining was assigned in random groups. The venue was completely dark. Participants used canes and listened to the voice of a waiter to guide themselves through the dark. When other participants first entered the room, I didn't feel anything. The moment I sat down in my chair and started hearing voices from different places without seeing anything, I felt a sense of momentary panic. I started talking to myself silently. *What am I doing here? This is the most ridiculous thing I have ever done!* I was about to stand up and ask for help to leave when, all of a sudden, one of my colleagues touched my hand and said, "Habib, I am here." Then I was connected to my group.

At the beginning, sitting in the dark was very foreign, very much outside my comfort zone. When my colleague connected with me through touch, I was less uncomfortable and somewhat reassured. I realized how important the sense of touch is. We generally take it for granted and never give it any sense of transcendance. I started adapting to the situation by touching the silverware, the plate, and even the food. Everything was a mystery—what to eat, how to eat, when there was something to eat. It was a unique, weird experience that I did not necessarily enjoy but found very revealing.

I believed dining in the dark took only 45 minutes, when actually it lasted almost two hours. I also related this experience to negotiation. When operating outside your comfort zone, you have the opportunity to both expand your skill set and practice what you know works. You can not only influence, but also transform the context so you can understand to be understood through the use of skills we seldom use in negotiating, such as touching. Fear of exploring new concepts and options robs us of growth possibilities. Sensory deprivation can actually make us more sensitive to the feelings of others. Thank God for your talents, but use them and explore the ones you haven't yet mastered.

Lessons learned in the negotiation process:

1. First recognize that each negotiation is different; despite preparation, we are functionally blind in new circumstances.
2. Second, realize that a negotiation can be a process of pressure and tension. Panic may trigger self-defense mechanisms and create barriers rather than bridges for communication.
3. Third, remember we have talents that surface in times of pressure that we often ignore or underemphasize (i.e., as in the case of touch in dinner in the dark). Even awareness can give us a competitive advantage.
4. Fourth, it is good to keep in mind the spontaneity in negotiation. Readiness will help us keep calm and take control of the negotiation.

5. Finally, adapt to situations and different contexts during the negotiation, as in the case of being completely blind, not knowing what to expect.

Through these two stories in which the "normal" context was transformed by silence and darkness, we discovered two very important conditions for a negotiation to transcend. The first one involves connecting with ourself and listening intently. The second is to create an environment that allows us to explore overlooked talents and use them as a springboard to sail in deeper waters at the very bottom of the iceberg (see the following illustration), and thus perhaps find a sense of being. Both conditions lead to the same discovery when we negotiate to enrich ourself. We enter into another dimension of relevance and another level of virtue (Lopez Quintas, 2003), unlike when we focus only on getting what we want and use the negotiation to meet an objective or outdeal the other party.

Next, we explore how to leave behind the idea to 'win at all cost' in a negotiation and enter into the realm of the transcendental.

Transcendental Negotiation

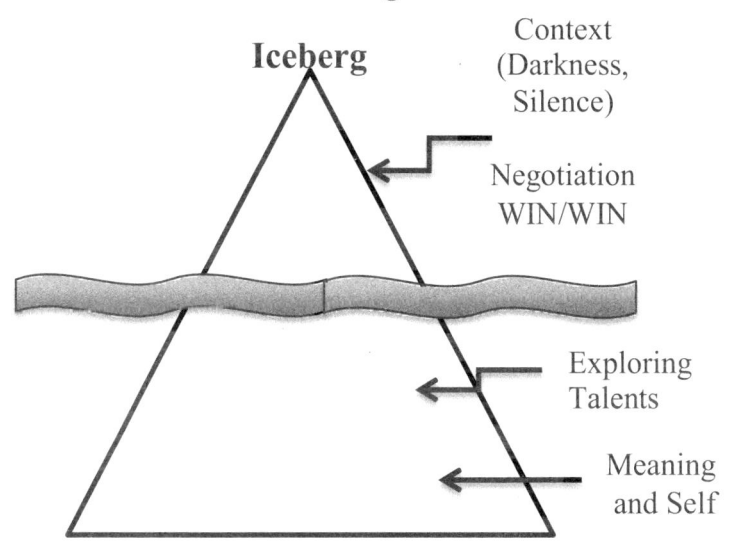

```
         Iceberg        Context
                        (Darkness,
                        Silence)

                      ← Negotiation
                        WIN/WIN

       ~~~~~~~~~~~~~~~~~~~~~~~~

                      ← Exploring
                        Talents

                      ← Meaning
                        and Self
```

This figure illustrates the passage of a transaction to a transcendental negotiation. A mere transaction remains on the tip of the iceberg. A transcendental negotiation is when we dare to swim in deeper water.

TRANSGENERATIONAL NEGOTIATION

A few years ago, I went with a group of graduate students from Houston to Europe. The trip was intended to explore the Phoenician route to Cadiz, Spain. Along the way, we also visited Toledo, Spain, where even today you can sense an atmosphere of tolerance and respect for cultural differences. There, we witnessed how Muslims, Christians and Jews lived in harmony and as a united community with respect that has been passed from generation to generation. To experience this cultural particularity, my students made in-situ real negotiation practices.

I especially remember my student John, who wanted to buy a souvenir from Toledo. He entered a local store and began a game of haggling with the owner. The piece of art cost 50 €, but John offered 25. The owner replied, "No way." John adjusted the offer to 26 €. The owner refused once again. The student made a counteroffer of 27 €, but the owner continued with the same answer until the offer reached 40 €. Then I stopped the process and privately asked John to ask the owner why it was not possible. The owner, smiling, confessed that he could not sell the piece because it had a small defect, but if John insisted, the owner could let him have it for 5 €.

There are very important lessons in that experience. The first is to listen and understand. The other is to find out why he is not agreeing to our offer, what his interests are, and what motivates or de-motivates him. Recall the story of the monastery: get into a deep silence, filter our noise, and listen to others. Understanding only follows questioning the shop owner's refusal to sell the piece, when the imperfection was unperceivable. What would the owner lose if he accepted John's first offer?

What would have happened when John noticed the defect in the piece upon arrival back home? He would be likely to think that the owner had deceived him. John should have thoroughly inspected the piece before making an offer. Why did the owner insist on not selling it without giving explanation? After purchase, the owner told us that to sell something in his store is to sell something that represents his community. If a traveler is dissatisfied and complains about price, quality, or anything, it will generate a bad image of Toledo for future customers.

"Would someone from Houston harbor ill feelings toward Toledo for buying a defective object years ago?" I asked the owner. "Precisely, that's what makes Toledo different. We care about our reputation." How many business people care more about the reputation of their community than generating profit? Surely, few. However, Toledo, which homes Jewish, Christian and Muslim communities, continues to uphold a commercial spirit of respect that transcends generations.

A transcendental negotiation is based on values and cultural principles. However, we cannot discover these negotiations unless we are silent in order to listen and ask the necessary questions to understand the dimension the other is negotiating. In short, the transcendental dimension of the owner was not the same as John, who was simply practicing the game of haggling.

*Toledo, Spain. Historical place of religious tolerance
Picture: Habib Chamoun-Farah.*

Additionally, each culture may operate naturally in a different negotiation dimension. John was in the dimension of objects interchanged or haggling, while the owner of the store was in a transgenerational dimension, which is similar to the negotiating culture of the Phoenicians.

"I AM SORRY, I AM GREEK"

The writer Amin Maalouf says that when a person feels lost, their identity is fragmented into "murderous identities"; however, when a person looks at his identity, he realizes that it is constructed of a mixture of several

```
                 Transgenerational
                 Dimension


                              Cultural
                              Dimension
         Haggling
         Dimension
```

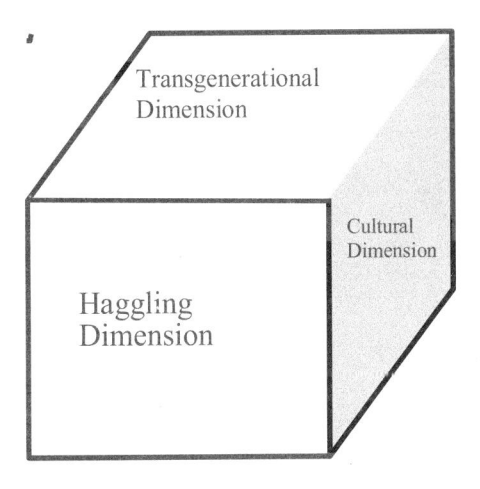

Perhaps different cultures negotiate in different dimensions.

identities and numerous affiliations that originate from various places. That is, that identity is the sum of a plurality of elements, and therefore, you can find a sense of belonging in a variety of experiences. What happened to me the first time I went to Greece has to do with what Maalouf says, as I was determined to find myself and others who, although we looked alike, were not.

The first time I was in Athens, I had a fantastic experience. From the first moment I made contact with the locals, it was very nice. People always spoke to me in Greek. I did not understand the language, but everyone, from the manager of the Greek airline to people on the street and in restaurants, was extremely friendly and very attentive. Their behavior made me feel more like another Greek. I connected immediately with them without any effort on my part. I experienced something very different from what happened to me in previous experiences where the context and conditions were unanticipated. In local stores, they gave me the same price as locals, rather than tourist prices given to other people I met on the trip.

I was afraid to speak, since they treated me nicely based upon my looks. I was wondering if I had a Greek past. Since everyone was so nice, I made a self-commitment to learn basic Greek words to be able to communicate and to provide feedback. After learning some common phrases, I went to the market to explore local negotiation processes and tactics. I learned how to say good morning (Kalimera), hello (Yazu), how much does it cost? (Posso Costi), thanks so much (Efaristo), as well as the numbers 1 to 10. For my minimal effort, I received a discount. I also learned how to say tourist price vs. local price. This was one place in the world I didn't need to negotiate very hard. I found out from my Greek friend that I looked like a famous Greek politician, which could work both ways; if he was liked, they would like me, but if he wasn't liked, then I could be in trouble.

I started reflecting on why Greek people were so nice to me in contrast with other places I had been, such as Jakarta, Narita, Hong Kong, Donetsk, Beijing, Malabo, Paris, Istanbul, Frankfort, Vienna, Berlin, Stuttgart, Mexico City, Buenos Aires, Quito, Bogota, Valencia, Cadiz, Bratislava, Rome, Florence, Pau, Sydney,

Moscow, Dublin, Cordova, Barcelona, and Madrid. While people are very nice and polite in all of the aforementioned cities, I easily met my negotiation objectives in Athens. Why? Of course, if you treat people nicely, most likely they will treat you nicely (Cialdini, 1993).

Before I even opened my mouth, the Greeks were nice and spoke to me in Greek. In a restaurant, I was served a more traditional homemade Greek plate rather than what tourists are typically served. Without haggling, I received 15 to 20% discount. In a market, I said, "Kalimera, posso costi." They replied, "Penda (10)." I countered, "Octo (8)", and I received it. I responded, "Efaristo kirie" (Thank you, sir). I didn't need to emphasize anything, whereas in Spanish, English or French, I might have been inclined to use more tactics to negotiate. Perhaps if I knew more Greek, I may have also tried to use more tactics.

Although the Greeks are known for their hospitality, it appears that the locals in Greece are treated better than foreigners. This is much different than my experience in Latin America, where foreigners receive better treatment than their fellow countrymen.

As I was walking in the center of Athens, I found a play with the English title *Sorry I am Greek!* but the play was in Greek. I asked a local about the meaning, expecting it to be sarcastic, e.g., *I am Greek, excuse me, we are great!*

The reply was exactly what I expected it to be. So if Greeks like Greeks, and you look Greek, then they will like you with an instant connection. Perhaps this connection during negotiations within a purchase is so nice and smooth that it creates confidence and immediate trust (Lewicki, 2003).

Among the lessons learned, we can observe that when in Rome we must not necessarily do as the Romans do in a negotiation. In other words, we must not imitate. Maybe doing nothing but observing and mimicking naturally is the key to connecting with a culture similar to ours, as was my case with the Greeks. Another lesson is that if you realize that you connect without a problem, then begin to understand the culture and act with respect and tolerance without imitating, there may be an undercurrent of reciprocity resulting in goodwill and favorable actions of another culture similar to ours. This encourages the recipient to act in a positive way. This will yield a negotiation with less tension between the parties.

In conclusion, we may find our identity and a sense of belonging in similar cultures. Perhaps this has to do with a spirit of abundance in the host culture. Cultures with this kind of spirit make the other feel important. Above all it fosters dignity, which shouldn't be lost in any business transaction. Otherwise, the host culture may lose both dignity and the business.

Identity is the sum of a plurality of elements and numerous affiliations that come from various places, according to the writer Maalouf. Perhaps Athens, Greece, is one of those places where my identity comes from.

CREATING A DESERT

On a splendid journey to the city of San Antonio, Texas, a sermon by the Archbishop of the city was very compelling. What impacted me most was an analogy made by the Archbishop between an arid desert and bleak situations of loneliness or peril. Out of necessity, people who live in the desert use every part of a resource and encourage others to do likewise. Otherwise, all would perish.

He observed that the ground is so dry West of San Antonio that networks of cracks form in water-starved soil. People living in this arid region use all available resources to survive under these conditions. Man becomes insignificant when you have everything. Creative solutions are often generated out of despair.

This experience of the desert reminded me of my dining experience in the dark while in Hong Kong. Paradoxically speaking, we need deserts in our lives to avoid paralysis of talents stemming from leisure and laziness, from abundance of materiality. Abundance is not bad provided it does not hinder "being."

It is recommended that a negotiator needs to experience the desert in order to develop their skills to be able to encourage and motivate the search for better solutions. Having resources is an important asset in any negotiation, but limited resources help us to use our creativity. The dilemma may be to have resources and lack the knowledge of how to live in the desert.

There are people living life to the fullest in the middle of the desert while others are in anguish to obtain resources.

In the desert, the need to use your talents comes to light. Such is the case in the parable of the ten virgins (Matthew 25:1-13):

At that time the kingdom of heaven will be like ten virgins who took their lamps and went out to meet the bridegroom. Five of them were foolish and five were wise. The foolish ones took their lamps but did not take any oil with them. The wise ones, however, took oil in jars along with their lamps. The bridegroom was a long time in coming, and they all became drowsy and fell asleep.

At midnight the cry rang out: 'Here's the bridegroom! Come out to meet him!'

"Then all the virgins woke up and trimmed their lamps. The foolish ones said to the wise, 'Give us some of your oil; our lamps are going out.'

"'No,' they replied, 'there may not be enough for both us and you. Instead, go to those who sell oil and buy some for yourselves.'

"But while they were on their way to buy the oil, the bridegroom arrived. The virgins who were ready went in with him to the wedding banquet. And the door was shut.

"Later the others also came. 'Lord, Lord,' they said, 'open the door for us!'

"But he replied, 'Truly I tell you, I don't know you.'

"Therefore, stay awake, for you know neither the day nor the hour.

Sometimes we have available resources, but only when the right situation presents itself do we discover their usefulness. There are times when our talents become an incentive for others to put theirs into practice. This is where we transcend the concept of winning the negotiation.

One day it occurred to one of my sons to invite his immediate family into a jogging competition. Initially, there were four of us, then we expanded to add other family members and friends. The objective was to run 50 km in 20 days, and the first to reach the distance would be the winner. For me, it was a challenge to compete against the faster teenager.

By using your talents you encourage others to use theirs.

To keep daily track of the race, we used a smart phone application that calculated and compared the progress of each competitor. I remember that on my first day, I ran half a kilometer, and my children held a five kilometer advantage. The next day, I ran three kilometers and continued increasing up to eight kilometers. I finished in second place. In the third race, I finished first. With over 30 years of age difference, less flexibility, strength and power, compared to teenagers, I won the race. What is the moral?

I learned that despite having a collaborative style in negotiations, I am very competitive. Once we organized a measureable challenge in which we were able to track our progress with respect to others, I was motivated to run a little more time and distance each day. Also, I took the initiative to run two kilometers more than whoever was in first place, knowing my actions might certainly motivate others to also improve their position. The effect was fabulous. In the competition, there was collaboration that generated a virtuous circle. My desire to remain in first place and ultimately win forced others to run more. It created a positive competition.

Another important catalyst in this challenge was the availability of a meter or indicator. When you are in a desert environment, as distance runners establish, you need motivation to achieve a measureable goal and overcome thoughts of giving up. This force is probably the same one that drives people living in the desert not to perish.

For me, the most important lessons in the desert were perseverance and discipline. As seen in my sports example, as in negotiations, goals and a visualized, tangible path to achieve those goals are necessary.

Perhaps we can extend these concepts to explain the longevity of monasteries, which continue to operate thanks to discipline and perseverance. Over 1500 years ago, the Benedictine monks focused on values of BEING rather than those of DOING or HAVING. In contrast, large corporations disappear or have to reinvent themselves not because they fail to set objectives, but because they pay insufficient attention to the path toward those goals. Great shortcomings of the modern world are derived from giving more importance to novelty than endurance. Enduring is worth more than adapting. It may be worth learning to negotiate against the current, serving more rather than getting. The fish that goes with the flow ends up in the nets of a fisherman. Those who swim against the current survive and become stronger.

BE TO TRANSCEND

I was invited along with other parent volunteers to my children's school to talk to students about my career. We were assembled to explain the roles, responsibilities and activities of each of our professions respectively. Our audience was small groups of eighth grade students with an average age of 14 years old. In preparation for the talks, we were warned that students could ask such indiscreet questions as "What is your salary, and why did you choose this career over another?"

Torrent ducks swimming in stormy streams countercurrent to survive.
Picture: Emile Chamoun-Farah.

In my presentation, I began by asking students what they wanted to be. I got the expected responses: doctor, engineer, nurse, teacher, etc. Then I asked them why. And they answered, "to have a lot of money," "to have a great car," "to have a big house," "to marry and have children." To this I replied that this question has challenged me all my life to understand what I'm doing and why. I finally understood my mission in life—to be personal and professional. I continued by describing my varied professional activities and my various titles: son, spouse, parent, researcher, consultant, salesman, teacher, business developer, and negotiator. Still, the most important for me was to "be" a father, husband and son. With this I showed television interviews and presentations that I had made promoting my book, *Negotiate Like a Phoenician*, in Latin America, Europe, and Africa. Some of the pictures of my trips showed my family and myself. With this, I noted two points. The first is that my work, despite being a sacrifice for my family due to the heavy travel schedule, is also fun since it often allows us to travel together. Rather than state my second point. I asked a question. If someone could guess what I had studied in college, they would win a book.

Everyone participated with great enthusiasm. They guessed that I was a lawyer, deputy, senator, public relations manager, and social worker—everything but what I actually studied. Since no one was right, I told them what I studied. It was the least expected, because very often, we tend to have a wrong perception or stereotype of careers and professional activities related to college majors. I studied to be a chemical engineer, added a business degree, then a master's and PhD, and I finally worked as a Postdoctoral Fellow. Academic pursuit is not as important as asking yourself why pursue this pathway.

In my case, it took me 40 years to discover why I did what I did. Year after year, I concluded I studied engineering because it was difficult and I liked the challenge. It took me 40 years to understand that careers in engineering and hard sciences seemed to help me open my mind and make me think and problem-solve in life's challenges, giving an advantage over alternative courses of study. Then I looked into the eyes of these students.

At a time when I knew I had everyone's undivided attention, I mentioned that in my life I've concentrated more in the "Being" than in the "Having" or "Doing". I invited those who said they wanted to be doctors, lawyers, nurses, and specialists to think and reflect upon their rationale. It is not bad that they want to have things like luxury cars and large homes, but they will be much happier if they focus more on Being and contentment with what they have than on setting their life direction toward "Having" or "Doing."

It was a great experience for me to share these thoughts with these eighth graders. To my surprise, the teachers called me to say that the children were highly motivated by my presentation, and I received many letters of thanks. We are in a time of chaos, where it is more important to focus on the "Being" than "Having" or "Doing". Look around you and think about what you're doing personally and professionally to contribute to others and share some of what you have. Then you can begin the path of a negotiator who transcends.

If we care to transcend as individuals and as negotiators, we must seek the essential, that which is "invisible to the eye", as the writer Antoine de Saint-Exupéry says in *The Little Prince*. The road is as important as the result.

Let us reiterate two fundamental questions for this book: How do I transcend as a negotiator? Is it possible to negotiate from faith?

The Latin-American Bible offers us a thought to reflect on:

> *We build with our faith, we build with our work, we build with our ability to understand others. But what it is built on the land is not the definitive. That is why God says: I will Trust you more. The Justice of the Kingdom and the dignity of man will be other riches to be distributed. We are working essentially in the little and God will establish the much.*

This construction, as noted at the beginning of this book, should be made on ethically and morally solid pillars if we would like to transcend.

The road and the objective are reflected in oneself.

NEGOTIATING WITH MEANING

> *Man is the one who questions man.*
> *The man infinitely surpasses man himself.*
> *The man is not the answer of himself;*
> *The man of yesterday and tomorrow is related to the man of today.*
> *Any man carries his ancestors within himself, and*
> *God never saves man without man, always with man, never against man.*
> Saint Augustine

A transcendent negotiation involves going to encounter others and leaving a positive mark on the world. However, the meaning of negotiation can also result in a misunderstanding, especially when one of the parties does not open to the possibility of transcending their own interests. This party is blind in his own vision, blocking the possibility of taking the relationship to a more humane end. We cannot impute this closeness to the lack of will; there are also cultural factors in which we are immersed that determine precisely the sense in which we approach every situation. One of these factors is what anthropologists call the "meaning of history". The meaning of history is the way in which a community explains its evolution in the world, in other words, how will the community answer questions such as "where am I, where do I go?" The response determines, to a large extent, the way in which that culture manages and negotiates available resources. Hence the subtitle of our book: *Quo vadis, negotiator*—where are you going, negotiator? What is the meaning of your negotiation?

Hernan Pereda Bullrich, in his book *Meaning of History*, takes up the thought of anthropologist Mircea Eliade to show that every civilization—and sometimes every person—answers these questions from a different conception. Pereda highlights three general conceptions:

The Quietist Conception is characterized by a rejection of the present, fear of the future, and negative judgment on everything new or innovative. The Quietist values only the immutable, the unchanging.

Every man brings within his ancestors. Saint Augustine
Schönbrunn Palace Gardens, Vienna, Austria

He wants to return to the "golden age" of his ancestors. It is encapsulated by the most classical "more certain" conception: "Better the devil you know than an unknown good." Actually, it is fatalistic in that it neither recognizes nor believes in history (see Figure 1). The events are interpreted as a function of a sacred law or a fixed myth.

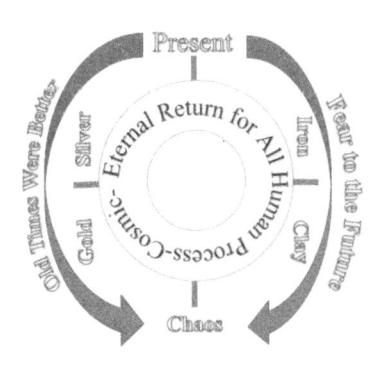

Figure 1. Quietist Conception

Revolutionary Conception is also characterized by a rejection of the present, but it further fears the past, negatively judging everything old. He is only interested in what is new and initiates perpetual change. He wants to create chaos to reach a new "golden age." This is the conception less frequently adopted, because it is more risky and less certain, but in reality, equally fatalistic. Talks about Re-evolution end up being a "twisted" involution (see Figure 2).

Linear Conception. If, however, we see the process of history as linear, everything makes sense and eventually finds its own meaning, what we call transcendent value, which is ultimately anthropological. Recalling the principles that man infinitely surpasses man himself, and man is not the answer of himself, we can conclude this requires both something superior to man, and the need for man to transcend (see Figure 3).

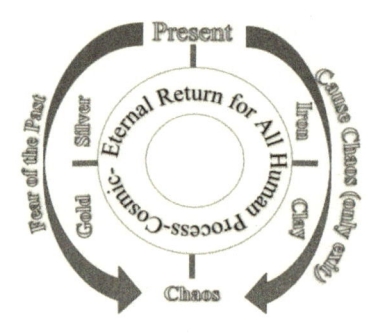

Figure 2. Revolutionary Conception

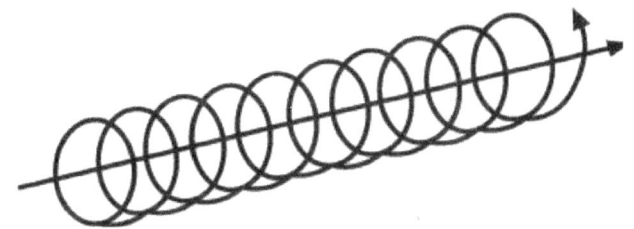

Figure 3. Linear Conception

As we can see, the quietist and revolutionary conceptions agree in rejecting the present and strive for a bygone or coming golden age, one from the static and the other through a perpetual motion. Both trace their way in a circular movement of history.

A simple way to understand the quietist circular view is to recall the history of Mexico. When Hernan Cortes appeared on the Gulf Coast, the Mesoamericans interpreted Cortes' arrival according to the myth of Quetzalcoatl. Hernan Cortes, however, was a man whose linear view of history allowed him to interpret every event as an opportunity to meet his target.

In a negotiation we can find people who have a circular vision. They live locked in an impasse, interpreting everything that happens in terms of their past or a future, and sooner or later they end up destroying themselves. If we look at ancient history, we find two cultures that formed the basis of a linear conception of history and, like the Phoenicians, have a good reputation as negotiators. We refer to the Jewish people and to their neighbors, the Phoenicians.

Both lived in a time when everything was interpreted in terms of laws and immovable myths (circular direction); however, there were events that triggered a new way of understanding history. The exodus out of Egypt of the Hebrew people, the appearance of the figure of Jesus Christ and the promise of resurrection put on the horizon two concepts that gave meaning to the existence of the People (where do I go?): The fullness and progressive human liberation. Meanwhile, the Phoenicians, great merchants, settled in their negotiations a sense that transcends this mere transaction. For them, it was essential to build relationships that would last over different generations, like the case of the business relationship of Jewish Kings David and Solomon with Phoenician King Hiram.

In both cases, the Phoenician and Hebrew are a forward projection that does not disdain the past. From this linear or progressive view of history, the existence of human beings takes a different and hopeful direction. In circular visions, the human being is exceeded by the mandates of the past or a future that does not end up becoming present. In linear vision, however, humans can leave a mark and build with the hope that what they do today will be beneficial and bring fullness to future generations.

In order to have a meaningful negotiation and avoid getting lost on the way to negotiate, we should act from a linear vision, since it allows us to interpret events as opportunities to create and build. This linear perspective invites us from the present to bring into play the available resources and transform them into opportunities for knowledge, especially since there is no business relationship that is perfect, because human relationships are not chemically perfect. What do I mean?

In my experience as a chemical engineer (my first career) I have learned that in a chemical equation, for a given reaction, we must put exact portions of each ingredient. The magic, the perfect result, also depends on the appropriate conditions of temperature and pressure. To some extent, even the most complex chemical equation is controllable and manageable. However, on a human level, although the relationship has all the ingredients required to produce a "magical" reaction, this may not happen, because our relations system is inherently flawed. But that's precisely what makes it interesting: the relationship management.

PHOENICIAN HERITAGE

If there is a civilization expert in human relations and negotiation, it is the Phoenician civilization. The Phoenicians have passed into history as the best traders in the world. They were famous for peacefully conquering the Mediterranean through a powerful and virtuous negotiating capacity. It is so surprising in this civilization that I don't hesitate to position them on the cusp of diplomatic and creative capacity.

Interestingly, great figures of the Phoenician history are remembered for these two skills. **King Hiram of Tyre** negotiated the construction of the temple of Solomon, the Hebrew king with whom he had a business relationship that extended from the time of **King David**. **Princess Elisa (Dido)**, founder of the city of Carthage, was a negotiator with great creativity. She managed to negotiate the exchange of the skin of a bull for all the land which constituted Carthage, territory that became the great Carthaginian Empire. **Prince Cadmus**, king of Tyre, is considered the first teacher of history, who brought the alphabet to the Greeks, probably with the intention of improving their trade relations. **Taautos** was a promoter of civilized life. He is considered the driving force behind the orderly ways of thinking, doing, relationship building, socializing and communicating. His teachings led to advancements of science, arts, law, society and religion. While the qualities of these characters have individual merit, they are also representative of a constructive and vital culture that is reflected in its model of negotiation:[1]

having the Phoenicians' commercial dealings with the great cultures of their time not only talk about the quality of their product but the correct way to distribute them. The transactions performed with Babylon, Yemen, Greece and Egypt gave the Phoenicians a reputation based on righteousness and trust. These same Phoenicians,

---

[1] The description of the Phoenician model corresponds to the one that makes Johnston (1965) and appears in the book *Negotiate Like a Phoenician*.

after several generations of practicing commerce, learned and realized that the best negotiation and trade policy was honesty, especially in the context of conflict in which they lived.

Phoenician Sarcophagus Cover in Human Shape, Century V& IV BCE., Sidon, Barracco Museum of Antique Sculpture, Rome.

The Phoenicians were the Canaanites that flourished around 1200 BCE., until the conquest of Alexander the Great in 332 BCE, even though the beginnings of this culture could go back as far as 2500 BCE (Sanford Holst, 2005). The Phoenicians learned to extract red, blue, and especially violet dyes from sea snails and mollusks. They recognized the market value of this prized product and understood their customers. The Phoenicians supplied the deep purple dyes to an elitist market—kings and royalty. The very name "Phoenicians" is derived from the Greek word *phoinikes*, or purple. In reference to themselves, they were Canaanites; to their customers, they were Phoenicians. Another of their natural resources was cedar, whose wood had a high demand among neighboring villages. To avoid being invaded, they convinced their contemporaries that a good long-term business relationship was more beneficial for everyone, since the Phoenicians had the largest merchant fleet at that time. Instead of focusing on one city, they founded small towns and ports in strategic locations to trade with major Mediterranean city-states. In addition to cedar, the Phoenician traded raw materials such as dyes, cotton, linen, glass, metals and even ivories. Their strategy didn't consist of competing with their neighbors for control of a product, but rather of making business partnerships with all practicing a philosophy with eight basic principles: have a solid product base, locate centrally, expand geographically, grow inventory, fill commodity and also retail markets, price fairly, deal honestly and always deliver the goods.

From this intercultural and mobile model, the Phoenicians did not see it as a compromise to their freedom, and became indispensable to the neighboring villages thanks to the ability of their merchant fleet. The port at Carthage is estimated to have housed 200 ships and each ship could transport more than 600 people. They also handled their relationships diplomatically. The Phoenicians were not interested in a military invasion of others to impose their culture. The stability of their business expansion depended upon their negotiating capacity, in addition to the proper protection of routes, caravans and ships in case of being attacked by robbers.

The region of Canaan, one of the most important Phoenician points, was chosen by the Israelites after their exodus from Egypt. To avoid corruption of their religion, the Israelites were to forcibly displace all people from the region. Army after army fell without survivor. The Phoenicians, however, remained and thrived as a culture. When Israel peaked in regional political dominance, so did the Phoenicians in terms of commerce. Israel had the wealth, and the Phoenicians had the goods. But not only that, the Phoenicians positioned themselves as trading partners of choice ,with a diverse product base and services; however, goods without salesmanship is not a working combination. The Phoenicians were great communicators. They created the phonetic alphabet that placed reading and writing in the hands of the masses.

Instead of practicing usury or manipulation, the Phoenicians maintained a trading philosophy based on the need for products and transparency of relationships. From them we can establish a legacy of seven principles of ethical and universal value (Sanford Holst, 2005):

- Create Partnerships. The Phoenicians sought that the transaction have benefits to their clients, in addition to generating benefits for themselves. The Phoenician chose their clients very carefully to ensure that the negotiation was implemented and enjoyed in peace.
- Trade Internationally. The Phoenicians' area of action was not limited; they always brought their ships to wherever the product was needed.
- Resolve Differences Peacefully. "Business is business" and nothing else. The Phoenicians refrained from making political alliances jeopardizing their business relationships.
- Express Religious Tolerance. Although they knew the religious beliefs of their clients, they never judged nor allowed them become an obstacle.
- Respect Women. The Phoenicians were very mindful of the fact that women were 50 percent of the market and that their decisions influenced the market behavior; treating their own women well allowed them to meet the needs of their women neighbors and clients.
- Uphold Equality. Despite living in a monarchy, the sense of equality was based on avoiding disputes and channeling all their energy and skills into negotiating.
- Retain Privacy (their own and their customers'). Respect private affairs so as not to take advantage or to manipulate the negotiation.

The Phoenician negotiation model transcended the environment of trade relations, since it was formed on a solid moral, constructive and vital basis. This also makes us understand how our method of negotiation repeats or rejects patterns of behavior of the times. Let us look at trade dynamics of today: while sellers act without scruples, the purest "*Lupus est homo homini*" style (wolf is man to man, phrase of Plautus popularized by Thomas Hobbes), consumers try to fill a certain emptiness from "*born to shop*", something like "I buy, therefore I exist". The senselessness and the current disorientation are due largely to the absence of an ethical base.

It is known that money has the ability to awaken, develop and turn the will in a powerful way. Although money is not a major factor to consider in a negotiation, without it, it would be impossible to carry out many projects. If we can guide that virtue to improve human life in our exchanges, we are working to become negotiators with meaning of transcendence, because negotiating is connecting people together for common ends. This relationship goes beyond the purely economic vision; in fact, it has more to do with the development of their own capabilities. To illustrate this in simpler way, let's recall the parable of the talents that appears in the book of Matthew in the New Testament:

Sometimes it is necessary to stop a little, look forward to discover the meaning of things and see where we are going.
Photo: Habib Chamoun-Farah

[14] "For it will be like a man going on a journey, who called his servants and entrusted to them his property. [15] To one he gave five talents, to another two, to another one, to each according to his ability. Then he went away. [16] He who had received the five talents went at once and traded with them, and he made five talents more. [17] So also he who had the two talents made two talents more. [18] But he who had received the one talent went and dug in the ground and hid his master's money. [19] Now after a long time the master of those servants came and settled accounts with them. [20] And he who had received the five talents came forward, bringing five talents more, saying, 'Master, you delivered to me five talents; here I have made five talents more.' [21] His master said to him, 'Well done, good and faithful

servant.[c] *You have been faithful over a little; I will set you over much. Enter into the joy of your master.' ²² And he also who had the two talents came forward, saying, 'Master, you delivered to me two talents; here I have made two talents more.' ²³ His master said to him, 'Well done, good and faithful servant. You have been faithful over a little; I will set you over much. Enter into the joy of your master.' ²⁴*

He also who had received the one talent came forward, saying, 'Master, I knew you to be a hard man, reaping where you did not sow, and gathering where you scattered no seed,²⁵ so I was afraid, and I went and hid your talent in the ground. Here you have what is yours.' ²⁶But his master answered him, 'You wicked and slothful servant! You knew that I reap where I have not sown and gather where I scattered no seed? ²⁷ Then you ought to have invested my money with the bankers, and at my coming I should have received what was my own with interest. ²⁸ So take the talent from him and give it to him who has the ten talents. ²⁹ For to everyone who has will more be given, and he will have an abundance. But from the one who has not, even what he has will be taken away. ³⁰ And cast the worthless servant into the outer darkness. In that place there will be weeping and gnashing of teeth.'

This parable reminds us that the talents received must be used in a way in which the human being stands before his own limitation and potential. As responsible negotiators, therefore, we have to use resources and our virtuous practices to give meaning to our negotiation activity.

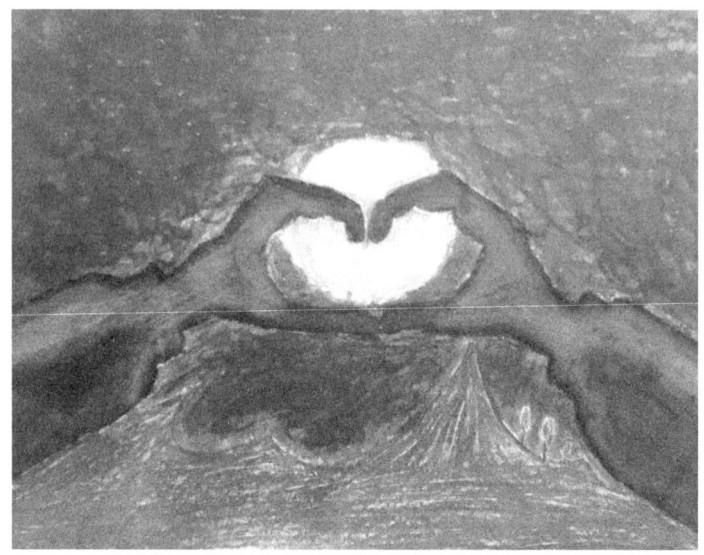

Man's heart is the engine of transcendence. Illustration:
Marcelle Chamoun-Farah

BARTERING, A CURRENT TOOL[2]

Although scholarly research has cleverly covered many types of negotiations, bartering has not been among the favorite topics for a profound analysis. Yet the United States Department of Commerce estimates that between 20 percent and 25 percent of all world commerce is done through barter. Corporate barter of tangible products and services is now a $20 billion industry (Mardak, 2002).

---

[2] Work taken from Chamoun, H., Hazlett, R., Valderrey, Fco, and Chiu, J. (2014). Bartering: When Negotiations Need a Creative Approach. *Tan Pan Chinese Journal of Negotiations,* 2(1).

In Hong Kong, during the days of hardship in the 1940s and 1950s, some benevolent doctors would accept whatever their poorer patients would bring (such as fresh fish or salted fish from the fishermen) in lieu of cash for their consultation fees and treatment. And today, while bartering has been considered by some to be an outdated way of trading, deals in military procurement, sales of premium technology products, commercial aircraft, and construction projects, among many others, when taken across borders, are prone to involve the exchange of services or physical goods instead of currency.

Bartering, therefore, is still active and should be seen as a mechanism to widen the set of alternatives of a negotiator; it may even be used in more modest settings, much closer to routine negotiations of almost any kind. More important, though, is to understand that bartering is one of the options available during the negotiation. Common to all these options is the belief that creativity may add solutions to those obtained by conventional means.

I remember one occasion when I was giving a lecture and one attendee asked me, "Tell me, Professor, do you practice negotiation or are you only an expert in theory?" To which I replied, "I have negotiated projects of several million dollars for companies where I worked, if that's what you mean."

At recess the participant approached me and asked me to help him with negotiation coaching for him and his management team. I had to brainstorm with his team to generate and review ideas needed to ensure that the negotiation of the sale of the company was on the right path.

I started working for this person with much enthusiasm and met with the management team. At the end of a two-day session, we concluded there was a lack of a plan B in the negotiations. In other words, if they did not reach an agreement on the sale of the company, what would be the plan B? We found out they didn't have a BATNA (Best Alternative to a Negotiated Agreement). The owner of the company was very happy with my work, particularly because by finding out they did not have a BATNA, they would generate a BATNA, thus increasing their bargaining power if they did not reach agreement with the customer. In closing the session, the owner turned to me and asked, "Habib, how much do we owe you?" While it is true that you have to be careful with the first offer of negotiation, because it can anchor the end result, you have to give a budget before starting the work. My big mistake was that we had begun work without a payment agreement.

I replied, 'Dear John, if I give you a price now that we're done working, it may be too high for you and you may feel committed to pay me my proposed amount because of the success of my work. I feel I made a mistake by not giving you a figure from the beginning, and we are now in an ethical dilemma, I think. You better tell me what you think it is a fair price. How much do you pay your lawyers in New York as a reference?"

'Habib, the dollar amount that I will propose is not going to be fair, probably will be very low and you have done a very good job. What do you propose?"

"Well, my dear John, we are in an ethical dilemma. If I give you a figure, it may be too high; you warn me that maybe yours is very low. What do you think if we generate an option? It occurs to me: within a month I have an event. I have been invited by the United Nations. I will be a speaker at an event where the President of the Republic will be attending. Your company could sponsor and donate to all attendees my new book *Negotiate Like a Phoenician*, and you don't have to pay me anything else. What do you think?"

John said, "I think it is a sensational idea. Very sharp and strategic. I have a budget for promotion. In addition, you have created a wealth for our company that we did not expect."

You are probably right if you are surprised this was a face to face conversation, too soft and indirect. Please reflect on your cross-cultural negotiation experiences where some communicate indirectly and others directly.

Many may criticize that my services where not valued because they were not paid and the book bartering gave greater benefits to John than to me. However, I ask you: what impact does it have that someone with prestige in the business world is sponsoring a book that will be donated to thousands of business people in an event with the President of the nation? Years passed, and when my beloved John was invited to Rice University in Houston as Keynote Speaker, he invited me, along with my wife Marcela, to sit at his table of honor. At his inaugural speech at the Houston Business Community, he said that everything that he learned to negotiate was through *Negotiate Like a Phoenician*, and showed the book to the audience.

How valuable is this academic testimonial and business reference from a Keynote Speaker at Rice University? Was it worth the bartering strategy? Of course, I have no doubt. So perhaps when we are in an impasse in a negotiation where the relationship is very important, consider bartering as an exit strategy. For the bartering to work, we must create value for both parties.

China, for example, has been helping some developing countries, especially in Africa, to construct buildings, transport systems (bridges, roads and railways) and mining industries, in exchange for diplomatic recognition and support in international organizations such as the United Nations. Cross-licensing of patents by high tech companies is another form of bartering, such as the case of the sale of the Motorola cell phone division by Google to Lenovo where Google kept most of the patents.

To illustrate how barter brings new options to the negotiating table, in 2014, my colleagues Hazlett, Valderrey Chiu and I presented in the *Chinese Journal of Negotiation: Tan Pan*, the case of an agreement between a consultant and a large organization. It was, first, a multicultural setting where a consensus was not reached.

In this multicultural scenario, no consensus is reached, and the impasse is only broken when mutual respect, personal reputation, and perceived common culture pave the road to a more personal relationship that allows unexpected solutions to be discovered.

While of an anecdotal nature, this case may serve as an invitation to understand the unique role that bartering proposals may (even when not ultimately accepted to close the deal) play in helping parties to bridge an impasse. In globalized markets, the background of the negotiators is more significant than ever. Although cultural diversity may become an obstacle, it should increasingly be used to find alternative solutions to deadlock scenarios.

Frequently, inter-firm relations encounter barriers; strategic approaches and technical expertise during the negotiation process may not be sufficient to provide viable solutions.

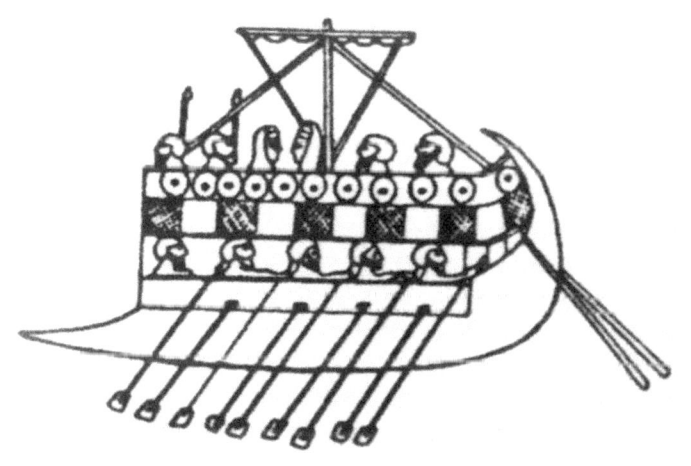

The barter system we inherited from ancient civilizations is a creative way to negotiate today.
Museum of Cadiz Phoenician Ship

If we follow the evolution of theories on this subject, we see that at an early stage, the skills of the people sitting at the table could determine the outcome of the negotiation. Today the paradigm is different, because knowledge and experience are just as important to mitigate the impact of personality traits and associated cultural origin or an individual's identity. However, alternatives such as barter are a good way to deal with the human dimension of a negotiation.

Bartering is often relegated in studies to underdeveloped economic systems predating the advent of common currency. Jack Kaikati (1976) argues that the famous economist Adam Smith criticized barter trade as a primitive, crude, and unrefined system of exchange. Indeed, barter, an exchange based upon equivalent worth, often has the problem of setting mutually agreeable values on items of contrasting size, measure, and utility; yet it represents the simplest picture of market-driven trade.

Barter is a naturally occurring societal phenomenon. As economies progress from self-sustaining agri-families, exchange for mutual benefit is predictable. One of the earliest accounts of cross-cultural bartering was documented by Herodotus in 440 BCE (Rawlinson, 1997), a case in which Phoenician traders placed transported goods on a beach for natives to exchange for local items of equal value. *Habib Chamoun and Randy Hazlett (2007) comment on the ability of the ancient Phoenicians to establish and maintain a mercantile network across multiple cultures despite a period of political unrest and cascading regional empire building.*

The Phoenicians certainly did not invent bartering, but through the use of technology, i.e., sea transport and navigation, they were able to connect regional resources to distant markets where greater value could be realized.

In another part of the world, beginning at the start of the Han Dynasty (139 BC), the famous Silk Road extended all the way from northwestern China to the Middle East (Damascus, and Alexandria), via Xinjiang and Persia. The Chinese would bring silk (hence the name Silk Road), lacquer utensils, iron products and herbs to the West (ending up in Rome via the Persian and Arabian merchants). In return, they would get some new species of fruits and vegetables (such as grapes, sesame, walnuts and green onions), exotic animals (such as the famous war horses from Central Asia, camels, lions, rhinoceroses, peacocks and ostriches), and valuables.

Also, around that time, in the Han Dynasty, there was the Sea Silk 'Road'. Ships travelled from southern China to India. From there other merchants would bring the goods all the way to Rome. The Chinese merchants exchanged their silk and gold products for spices, as well as pearls and other exotic valuables from the seas. The volume of goods exchanged was much larger than that of the land Silk Road, because of the much larger carrying capacity of the ships compared with that of the camel trains. Even in the Han Dynasty, it is estimated that the larger ships could carry 50 to 60 tons of goods (Editorial Committee, 2000). Thus bartering, an exchange of goods of equal local worth, was at the heart of the Phoenician business model as well as in the Chinese culture.

Indeed, there were exchanges for silver where value was established and accepted. The Phoenicians established a commerce system that linked established markets, connecting local goods to non-local markets through shipping and so-called trading posts. This certainly involved an exchange of goods in abundance for those in demand on a scale sufficient to require a mercantile fleet.

According to Feleke Tadele (2000), barter should be an important theoretical concept in economic anthropology. One could learn much from the historical social, cultural, and political forces that drive markets toward use of currency. The Phoenician society is especially interesting, as it spans the age of pure bartering into that of regionally accepted currency. Confronted with the ever-present problem of establishing worth in every bartering arrangement, some economies used a single commodity to establish relative value of all other goods as a precursor to currency. Magnus Widell (2005) envisioned two exchange systems in the ancient economies of the Ur III period: a barter system based upon the value of barley and a second based upon silver. Haydée Quiroz Malca (2009) described how indigenous communities from Guerrero, Mexico, have been trading since the beginning of their civilization in a bartering economy based upon salt. These are but a few isolated examples of evolving mercantile systems originating from barter. The Chinese used seashells as money in the ancient days.

As outlined by Tadele, anthropologists and economists list four characteristics inherent to barter:

1. Exchange is driven by mutual interest in goods with direct consumption value and derived satisfaction in the deal. We can see an example of this feature in Mexico's indigenous towns. In the state of Oaxaca, to

date the salt is exchanged for a product that indigenous groups need, say, a shirt. Bartering is driven by a mutual interest: people who exchange the shirt for the equivalent in grams of salt have an interest in salt, and the salt providers need or have an interest in this garment that surely cannot be produced in their community.
2. Trade is governed by internal balance of value in the absence of preset exchange rates. Suppose a barter of five shirts is exchanged for twenty-five kilos of salt. Where there is an absence of a common currency, the transaction is governed by the value that carries the object (shirt or salt) or per unit of weight in shirts / weight of salt. The key issue is to determine the value of the objects exchanged in barter.
3. Barter requires an interface with information on goods available to interested parties. To justify the value of an object two criteria are taken into account: the information provided about the product and how it is presented. It is not the same exchange for a linen shirt and one made of cotton. Those involved in the exchange must provide sufficient information to justify the value of the difference.
4. Barter creates social bonds, including isolated, discontinuous relationships, recurring exchanges, and relationships across widely varying socioeconomic and political groups, and it fosters good feelings between parties due to an inherent equivalency principle and the satisfaction that comes from a sense of fairness (Tadele, 2000). When customers bring novelties, toys or food to share with other individuals with whom they had already exchanged in the past, if the barter occurs in a context of tolerance and respect, as time goes on long-term relationships are created. In the case of the Phoenicians, who conquered the

Mediterranean without war and through trade relations, intercultural relations were created that lasted a period of 2000 years.

An alternative viewpoint recognizes barter not just as a historical institution, but as a contemporary phenomenon still much in use, though it is often disguised in alternate terminology. Kaikati also classifies four types of current international barter deals: (a) clearing agreements, (b) switch trading, (c) parallel barter, and (d) buyback barter. He also categorizes three types of domestic barter deals negotiated frequently today: (a) straight barter, (b) reverse reciprocity, and (c) advertising-media barter. According to Don Mardak,[9] more than one-third of all U.S. businesses engage in some form of barter, and 65 % of the companies listed on the New York Stock Exchange use barter to reduce inventory, bolster sales, and ensure capacity at production facilities (Mardak 2002). Barter and bartering networks enable organizations of all sizes to creatively manage their inventory in the face of constantly shifting supply and demand factors, adding value to supplies of otherwise diminished worth. According to Michael Gershman the advantages of bartering can be grouped under three headings: finance, purchasing, and marketing (1986). There is an advantage to moving the inventory of your goods for trade, to promote or market a new product or a new market among others. As a modern example, Darren Dahel cites an exchange of company equity for online marketing efforts predicated upon enhancement of easily definable company metrics (2010). This is essentially a barter of expertise for a share in the enhanced business. Tadele asserts that there can be few economies operating without barter (Tadele, 2000; Karen and Shera Dalin, 2010, Cohen, 2009). Given the economic downturn, people are reverting to the ancient form of commerce.

Transcendental negotiation is still possible with the use of barter; thus, we give importance to barter in this context, since it can meet needs that go beyond a simple trade. However, bartering should be considered for what it brings to the table beyond the mere exchange of objects, as it appears on the surface, in search for a means of transcendence.

CHAPTER II
PRUDENCE

Prudence is the virtue of practical reason that allows us to discern our true good and to choose the right means. San Gimignano, Italy

Picture: Habib Chamoun-Farah

WHAT DO WE MEAN BY PRUDENCE?

A couple of years ago, on a family weekend, one of my sons gave me a great lesson in prudence. I remember we got to the movies as a family and we managed not to agree on a movie, then I started negotiating with my children. Everything was fine until one of them made a comment that bothered me. Instead of taking a break and reasoning with him to achieve a viable solution, such as choosing a movie objectively, I responded aggressively. Another of my children, once he realized what was happening, turned on his mediating intelligence and with the right words showed us the advantages of one film over another. After buying the tickets, he approached me and told me that I had gone too far with my scolding; it was a family weekend and was not worth it to confront each other. On that occasion, thanks to him, I understood firsthand what it means to be prudent.

Prudence is the virtue that disposes practical reason to discern our true good in every circumstance and to choose the right means. The exercise of virtue is an exercise of reason and the will that takes place in any circumstance and in any historical or life situation that makes it possible to find the true good and to choose the means that leads us to it. So there is no good or bad situation; there is good or bad exercise of practical reason. What we need to ensure is that in the righteousness of the action, as St. Thomas of Aquinas, great master of virtues, says in the Summa Theologica (STH2-2 , 47.2), prudence is the rule of right action.

This should not be confused with either shyness or fear, or with duplicity or dissimulation; rather, the prudent one is not the one that bends, but he who uses reason in any situation. Thanks to prudence, I can apply moral principles without mistake in particular cases of negotiation, and thus overcome any doubt about the good that I must do and the evil I must avoid.

In that sense, prudence is not just a restrictive virtue but also an encouraging one, i.e., besides helping to clarify the boundaries of good and evil, it also allows us to imagine the actions that are possible within that framework. So knowing when to take a risk is a result and an attitude of prudence.

The word *prudence* comes from the Latin *prudentia*, which proceeds also from *pro Videntia*, meaning 'who sees in advance.' Perhaps that is why we have heard that prudence is the mother of all virtues, because it not only gives us the willingness to understand the circumstances, it also leads us to act or create—the negotiation is the creation of a new possibility—the fundamental conditions of justice, fortitude and temperance. Only the one who is prudent can be wise, fair, strong and temperate. The imprudent, however, is far from being fair and strong, as his "courage" actually responds to a personal and highly subjective interest. From this perspective, a negotiation doesn't consist of managing the circumstances for an individual goal; moreover, it doesn't count the "good intention" or the "goodwill" to launch a negotiation process.

What counts is to carry out the good, fundamental motivation in all transcendental negotiations. This makes our action depend on the pursuit of a common good in real and practical situations. This requires that we pay attention, with rigor and objectivity, to the realities around us.

COLLABORATIVE NEGOTIATION

Prudence is a form of practical wisdom that allows us to act in the best way to achieve a particular purpose. Like the rest of the virtues and practical knowledge, prudence is developed and perfected from the experiences and lessons it gives us. As a professor, I have always sought ways to provide my students' experiences and methodologies aimed at forming negotiators with ethical sense. One of these experiences came while I was professor of International Business and Marketing at the Universidad del Istmo in Guatemala.

For sixteen weeks I worked with senior students in implementing a model of collaborative negotiation. The objective was simple: **to Carry out Good** in their homes or work.

Students had to work together to improve coexistence with a family member or with a coworker or boss they didn't get along well with, but could not tell anyone why they were doing this work. During the semester, both in person and through e-learning (using the Skype application and Blackboard Collaborate platform), Professor Ana Izabel Matta Vega de Palacios and I were incorporating in the course a number of support tools, including the *Tradeables™* method. This method consists of identifying which factors create greater negotiating power for our present and future agreements. Among these factors are ideas and actions that drive the agreement without being part of the transaction,

Doing well without expecting anything in return brings greater benefits than expecting something. Antigua, Guatemala

or products and services that meet the needs of customers who are not in our product line and are not in competition with our offer. In a following section we devote more time exploring this method.

The students we worked with were an average of 20 years of age, socioeconomic level upper class, and most were still living with their parents. The first day we asked, "What do you do at home to help your family?" Most answered that they did nothing, not even simple tasks such as washing dishes, making the bed or walking the dog. We asked them to put into practice the model Tradeables at home without expecting anything in return and to observe if there were changes in their behavior or their family. In parallel, negotiations on video were analyzed based on their intuition and compared with what they learned in class.

These activities generated rich debates in class and enhanced the willingness and motivation to learn. Role-plays and cases were used to bring the best practices of worldwide negotiators. Among the things they learned was to negotiate via e-mail and chat by learning how to write messages, collaborating in a diplomatic way (asking questions, verifying, proposing and confirming) rather than competing or avoiding conflict. The negotiation tactics were explored so the students learned how to apply and counteract tactics with the objective of bringing the sides to agreement. Once students learned a set of negotiation premises and principles, they were told to apply these on a daily basis and bring their results for the next session.

The students were not only invited to apply simple negotiation concepts in daily activities, but also to look for creative ways of changing their negotiation behavior from avoiding or competing to being more collaborative by generating *Tradeables*. From the testimonials collected at the end of sixteen weeks, we noticed behavioral changes not only in students but also in the family or work colleagues. Thanks to a questionnaire filled at the beginning and end of the semester, we evaluated the effectiveness of negotiation based on the degree of collaboration and preparation, as well as how to understand competitors in a given situation, among other factors. Students also performed the Thomas Kilmann test in order to find a style of conflict management. Compared to other similar age groups and socioeconomic statuses in Mexico, Guatemalans were higher in the style to avoid. Interestingly, only two Guatemalan students held an initial collaboration dominant style; both had more work experience than the rest of the group and were older than average.

According to the daily reports, students who previously hadn't spent time on housework began to generate *tradeables* with their parents as a result of a change in behavior to be more collaborative. At least 20 of the 49 students changed their behavior. The testimonials of parents, colleagues and friends confirmed a significant increase in cooperative behavior.

Quantified improvement of student behavior suggests that by practicing the concepts taught in class to "carry out good" and by periodically having the students critically reflect upon what was done during class and real life negotiations and opportunities for improvement, negotiation skills learning effects behavioral change, even when change is opposed by cultural norms.

The most interesting result is that parents, friends, family or co-workers realized the change in behavior; most respondents reported a more collaborative behavior. Another interesting fact is that students also noticed a more collaborative treatment of the other party in reaction to its own collaborative action. In conclusion, recourse to *Tradeables*™ in the experiment of housework chores, unsolicited, improved the probability of mutually collaborative behavior.[3]

Here we share some of the testimonies gathered during this experience.

---

[3] Interestingly, when analyzing these results with my colleague Randy Hazlett we integrated some factors of game theory. As a result, we found that *Tradeables* can accelerate the approach to a Nash equilibrium, if one exists, and change the equilibrium position, topics discussed in depth later.

Student testimonials

After taking the course, my behavior showed several changes. Of the most important I might mention that now it has become a habit to seek information, to know what happens and how it affects other external factors. Now I consider that having a context of the situation allows me to reach the best conclusions and to adopt the best strategies. I also noticed that now I don't try to expose my position to others, but I choose to listen and observe how others react to what happens, because then you can understand how much importance or influence to ascribe to the person. Another behavior that I have changed is that now I do not give up easily with tough negotiators. Now that I know plenty of negotiation tactics and strategies, I think I have several tools to understand their best behavior and respond with alternative solutions. Always under the principle of a fair negotiation, I seek to exercise my power and ensure to establish my position in the negotiations.

Student 1

I must say that from the beginning of this course to its end, it has changed my behavior, especially with my family because often when I attempted to negotiate I did not always attain a positive result. This course helped me more than anything with my sisters to carry out good negotiations with them from the simplest things, always taking into account my interests and also the interest that any of them had about something specific. I take into account the concept of listening first and finding out what position one of them is in, and then placing a good proposal about how to solve something or simply come to an agreement. There was a change in attitude more than anything along this course. I could develop in a better way, which I will continue using in the course of my personal and professional life.

Student 2

As for the course, I've changed the way I ask for things in my house with my parents, either when asking permission or performing more things. At first they may not have realized it but then they noticed it, initially they believed that I wanted something in return or that something was wrong with me. I wanted to work more in the house for my parents and they finally realized that I was doing it without expecting anything in return.

Student 3

After the course, I realized that I usually consider the benefits of others before acting. I reason more and I'm much more collaborative in many ways. I am more patient and I pay more attention to other people's opinions. I recommend the course to other students, because one learns many things that are put into practice in real life, while you learn to negotiate in different ways, using tactics to achieve the objectives.

Student 4

Third party testimonials

I think my sister changed a lot because now when I ask for something she understands me and does not question me as before. Now she finds the way to reach an agreement so that our relationship is going well. Now she is my friend and I can trust her because I know that now she likes to know that I am well, and if she does not like something she talks to me calmly, tells me her reasons and so it is easier to understand.

Sibling

It's amazing how my daughter has changed throughout this semester. Now she takes the time to understand others, to analyze the responses of others and not give answers without thinking of the consequences they might bring. Now we have the opportunity to share with her at the table and talk about various topics; previously it was impossible, as she was rigid in her posture and mindset about things. The change has been drastic. Now she advises me and makes both my husband and me see things in a different way, so that we can find out what is more convenient. I'm also very impressed, as her contributions to the house are quite visible, which means it helps the employees, and she makes her own breakfast and dinner and arranges her bedroom. She has become more helpful around the house and now we enjoy a peaceful environment.

Mother 1

I noticed some improvements in her behavior. Now she is more likely to help, and she is less introverted, has gained greater confidence in what she knows and her ability to negotiate improved. She has lost fear and felt no shame in asking for something. When she negotiates, she thinks more about what she can give to the other person. She also thinks about what she wants to achieve and how she can link what she wants with what this other person wants. Even when she comes with me to the market to shop, she shows me how I have to get the seller to give me a better price, and in the family business she shows me how to make our customers feel that we are offering something more than just a product.

Mother 2

TRADEABLES AND PRUDENCE IN NEGOTIATION

After exploring the above case, surely you will wonder how and why *tradeables* can be a way to exercise prudence in negotiations.

As we mentioned previously in this book, *tradeables* can be:
a) A set of ideas or actions that help leverage a DEAL without being a part of the deal, or
b) Products and services that satisfy customer needs outside our own product line that are not in competition with our offerings.

Tradeables™ are, in fact, things that create greater negotiation capacity for our own present or future DEALs. *Tradeables*™ literally means "able" to "trade" or bringing trading capacity. Interestingly, if we extract the word DEAL from Tradeables™, we are left with *Trabes*, which in Latin means the beam or the structure of the DEAL.

Based on this curious game, we will explore the advantages that the *Tradeables* ™ model provides to improve the outcome of our negotiations.

In carrying out an agreement it must be recognized what is not negotiable, what is negotiable and what does not need to be negotiated. This is the first step to ensure optimal results. Such simple preparation minimizes waste of resources. However, there are other *tradeables* that can make a deal happen, even without focusing on the essence of the deal.

My colleague Randy Hazlett and I have proven that the concept of *tradeables* is not new, since it was a commercial practice of the ancient Phoenicians who built and managed a trade empire spanning several millennia amidst regional strikes and a history of conquest. The Phoenicians dominated sea trade around the Mediterranean for well over 2000 years, until the conquest of Tyre by Alexander the Great in 332 BCE. Phoenician influence continued without a central hub in Phoenicia proper, at least through the Punic Wars, through a network of established trading outposts.

Though the Phoenicians developed superiority in shipbuilding (Secrets of Archaeology DVD, 2003) and navigation (Herodotus, 1997), the advantage of technology alone could not account for the longevity of this mercantile society. Thomas Johnston deduced, "The mere fact that the main trend of the business of the Phoenicians was always toward the great centers of civilization makes it apparent that it was not only on account of the quality of their goods but equally on account of their manner of disposing of them that they were highly approved" (Johnston, 1965, p. 74). Hazlett and I speculate that the Phoenician business model enabled them to thrive in perilous times, with *Tradeables* playing a central role. Concerning gifts of appeasement offered to Assyrian king Tiglatpileser in roughly 875 BCE, Moscati (1969, p. 16) stated, "The Phoenician cities do not seem to offer any armed resistance, and there is no mention of battle. This would be in character with the traditional policy of the small states, which is to satisfy their powerful neighbors with homages and tributes." The Hebrew Scriptures give an extended account of dealings between King Hiram of Tyre and Kings David and Solomon, including a long history of unsolicited gifting and open agreements. The longevity of the Phoenician mercantile culture may also, in part, be attributable to intergenerational benevolence, as described by Wade-Benzoni (2006).

A word of caution: *Tradeables*™ are not "favors" with expectation of one in return. The common saying "I'll scratch your back if you scratch mine" does not apply. Such *quid pro quo* actions do not qualify as *Tradeables*™. The use of *Tradeables*™ should never be construed from either side as a bribe. As we shall see, the Phoenician business model is one of openness, fairness, and integrity. It elevates the customer as a long-term business partner ahead of the present DEAL. Any offer outside this framework simply is not in alignment with the spirit of *Tradeables*™.

THE PHILOSOPHY OF GIVING[5]

Another chapter of knowledge that precedes the concept of *Tradeables* is the philosophy of giving a central concept, found in the teachings of St. Thomas Aquinas, dating from the thirteenth century A.D., which places the common good above individual benefits. However, in the context of a negotiation, if we are not prudent, putting the common good first, prior to finding out the needs of each person, can create a negative atmosphere rather than a constructive one, especially in an intercultural meeting. For example, if the recipient of a *tradeable* comes from a different culture than the giver, maybe receiving a gift can be interpreted as a bribe or a form of manipulation. "A person can trigger a feeling of indebtedness by doing us an uninvited favor" (Cialdini, 1993). The need to return the favor with something of equal or greater value can be a powerful force in gaining influence or compliance.

In certain Hispanic cultures, gifting can set a precedent, and generous behavior can become an expectation, losing its power to create leverage. In fact, an unfulfilled expectation of greater giving will have negative consequences for both parties.

---

[5] Extract of the works realized with Randy Hazlett: 'The Psychology of Giving and Its Effect on Negotiation', *Rethinking Negotiation Teaching: Innovations for Context and Culture*, edited by C. Honeyman, J. Coben, and G. DePalo; St. Paul, MN: DRI Press, 2009.

In Middle Eastern cultures, giving is countered with reciprocity in excess. In a culture where refusal of gifts is actually insulting, giving can escalate to unwarranted levels. Others will interact with distrust until any hint of an ulterior motive can be laid to rest. Thus, there is risk in giving, especially for the unprepared negotiator. Even in culturally sensitive situations, if in the process of new data gathering giving is eventually construed as a sign of caring, then tremendous leverage exists for future dealings. If giving is without condition, non-manipulative, and unselfish, it will create great leverage for future interchanges among the parties. This will make a giver an effective giver, similar to an effective negotiator. Such giving makes both parties feel good. The giver feels self-affirmed, and the receiver feels appreciated. The persuasive power in giving is high. In the end, the one that gives the most gets to win the most.

To understand the complexity and the potential for a *tradeable*, let's explore the book *Grandeza de la vida* (2003), where Professor López Quintás explains that the interaction between objects, individuals and environments can elevate the levels of conduct and reality.

Level one consists of objects without possibilities, where objects can be used, exchanged, and discarded. This is the level of tangibles without interpretation—concrete reality. In level two, the level of ambience, objects hold capacity to shape their environment and can create possibilities. In order for possibilities to crystallize on this level, an encounter must take place between an interpreter and the ambience. If the interpreter has good intentions, i.e., a set of honorable values and principles, the level could continue rising to higher levels of meaning. However, if the interpreter uses the possibilities to his or her own advantage, this will generate negative levels, leading to destruction.

Professor Quintás brilliantly exemplifies this philosophy with a piece of sheet music – Ludwig van Beethoven's *Für Elise*. In the level of objects, the sheet music is simply a piece of paper without possibilities and is not the piece *Für Elise*. On the second level, however, the music sheet converts into an ambience capable of creating multiple possibilities. These possibilities require an encounter between the ambience (music sheet) and an interpreter. If the interpreter is well trained with a set of values, great music could ensue. A trained musician can even hear without sound, as the transcribed notes are no longer ink stains on paper. With the aid of another transformed object, a piano, even the untrained can experience *Für Elise*. Written music also contains dynamics—those marks of expression intended by the composer. A piece played well will honor all the notes and expression.

However, a great pianist will also add embellishment to the interpretation from knowledge of the composer, the musical style, or personal taste, transcending the sheet music to even higher levels.

If we analyze the Phoenician negotiation model with

more detail and profound reasoning, we find that the best practices of successful negotiators entertained Quintás levels superior to one, generating long-lasting relationships. In the concept of *Tradeables*, level one represents a simple exchange of objects outside of a trade, barter, or business transaction. Some cannot see the value in giving something away. They see this process simply as a change in inventory of objects. By contrast, in level two, *Tradeables* become ambiences capable of producing possibilities. If given in a spirit of caring, the object carries meaning and value greater than the object. *Tradeables* transcend from objects to symbols of relationship. If given in a spirit of manipulation, *Tradeables* can be ineffective and potentially negative to the business relationship. The skillful use of *Tradeables* as expressions of value in a long-term relationship promotes possibilities for future business the Phoenician way. Professor Quintás' levels of conduct and reality can actually give us a means for evaluating the effectiveness of *Tradeables* from the client's perspective.

WHAT ARE THE NEEDS OF MY CLIENT?

So far we have concentrated on the motivations of the negotiator. We have explored the importance of giving an ethical meaning to the negotiator's activity and put ourselves to practice in the first pillar, prudence, with tools that have proven effective in family life. Now let's talk about prudence to interact and relate with a customer, because you have to interact with the other in order to understand his needs. Tools and models are very useful to analyze and observe the potential rehabilitation of relationships. Relationships, in turn, are built through interpersonal communications. Johari Window (Luft and Ingham, 1955) is a psychological tool to help understand interpersonal communications.

This is why my colleague Randy Hazlett and I have captured the customer needs in this psychological tool. In addition to prioritizing the needs, it helps us determine the depth of the donor or the level of satisfaction, that is, it allows us to anticipate the potential benefits that will bring the *Tradeables*.

The traditional use of the Johari Window deals with personality traits. The tool, illustrated in Figure 4, distinguishes between personality elements known and unknown to either or both parties.

A similar segmentation can be performed on objects other than adjectives describing a person's conscious or subconscious behavior. In particular, we choose to map client needs onto a Johari framework as seen in Figure 5.

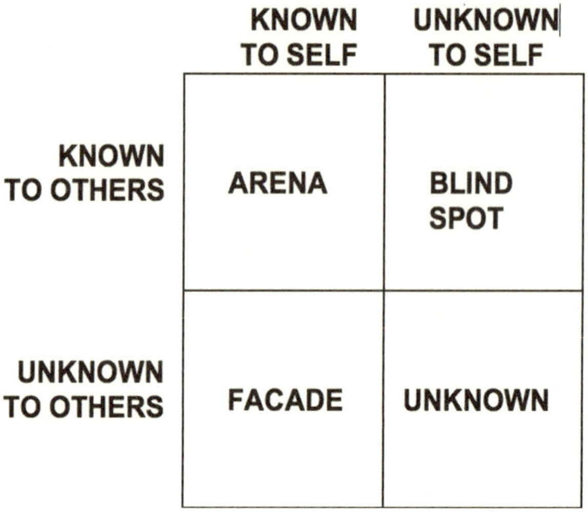

	KNOWN TO SELF	UNKNOWN TO SELF
KNOWN TO OTHERS	ARENA	BLIND SPOT
UNKNOWN TO OTHERS	FACADE	UNKNOWN

Figure 4. Normal Johari Window—A Psychological Tool for Interpersonal Communication (Luft and Ingham, 1955).

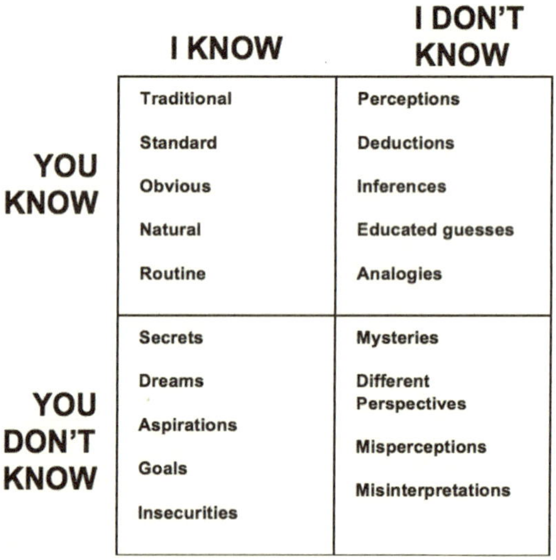

	I KNOW	I DON'T KNOW
YOU KNOW	Traditional Standard Obvious Natural Routine	Perceptions Deductions Inferences Educated guesses Analogies
YOU DON'T KNOW	Secrets Dreams Aspirations Goals Insecurities	Mysteries Different Perspectives Misperceptions Misinterpretations

Figure 5. Needs analysis in a Johari framework.

There are those needs that are known by both parties. These needs are traditional, standard, obvious, natural, or routine. You sell widgets; he needs widgets. There is a direct business connection. There can also be needs of the client which are unexpressed. These can include secrets, dreams, aspirations, goals, or insecurities. For whatever reason, the client has chosen not to reveal these needs. The client may be leery of sharing too much information, or he may believe you personally cannot—or are not in a position to—meet those needs. In certain relationships, such as those involving legal matters, the standard practice of leveraging facts and information to one-sided advantage regardless of implications creates an undercurrent of danger in disclosure (Caplan, 2004). There can also be needs that the client is unaware he has, but which can be reasonably known through perceptions, deductions, inferences, educated guesses, or use of analogies. (For example, Client A and Client B are companies with a similar product line, so they probably have similar needs.) Finally, there are needs which are unknown to you and the client. These could be "mysteries," wrong perspectives, misconceptions, or misinterpretations. Additional information or an investigative process could reveal these needs to one or both parties.

If we adjust the category names slightly from knowing to recognition, we can better interpret some needs. We can, in fact, categorize the meeting of needs in the various windows as Service, Benevolence, Ministry, or Therapy (see Figure 6).

	I RECOGNIZE	I DON'T RECOGNIZE
YOU RECOGNIZE	**SERVICE** Traditional Standard Obvious Natural Routine	**BENEVOLENCE** Perceptions Deductions Inferences Educated guesses Analogies
YOU DON'T RECOGNIZE	**MINISTRY** Secrets Dreams Aspirations Goals Insecurities	**THERAPY** Mysteries Different Perspectives Misperceptions Misinterpretations

Figure 6. Needs Classification and the meeting of those needs in a modified Johari framework.

Of course, it would be difficult to accidentally meet needs which never go recognized. As such, we speak of the category the need resided in initially. For example, once an undisclosed need known to the client is exposed, you may be able to address that newly discovered need. The need transitions from the Facade to the Arena window, and if met, we call that a Ministry. You addressed a deeper concern after gaining rapport and trust. Alternatively, you but not the client could have recognized the need. Meeting a need the client did not initially know he had is a gift—Benevolence. Meeting a need initially unknown to both parties is Therapy. We can also label the role of the giver in the meeting of needs from various categories (see Figure 7).

	I RECOGNIZE	I DON'T RECOGNIZE
YOU RECOGNIZE	**SERVANT** Traditional Standard Obvious Natural Routine	**BENEFACTOR** Perceptions Deductions Inferences Educated guesses Analogies
YOU DON'T RECOGNIZE	**CONFIDANT** Secrets Dreams Aspirations Goals Insecurities	**COUNSELOR** Mysteries Different Perspectives Misperceptions Misinterpretations

Figure. 7 Roles of the Giver

If you meet a service need you are a Servant. In doing the work of Benevolence, we have a Benefactor. This could likewise be a Teacher, Mentor, or Coach, depending upon situational status. The Benefactor is able to see the need and convince the client the need is real and theirs. Thus, meeting the need is like giving a surprise gift. In Roy Lewicki's (2003) dimensions of trustworthy behavior, levels of trust build with assessment of ability, integrity or acting according to acceptable principles, and benevolence—concern for the welfare of others.

A Confidant performs the work of Ministry. This is the person who gains trust to carry the relationship to a higher level of sharing. Finally, a Counselor does the work of Therapy. Through a process, they can embark on a joint venture to discover needs, validate them, and seek ways to address them. In a religious context, these might be replaced with the traditional roles of Servant, Preacher, Priest, and Evangelist.

There are also different emotional attachments to the meeting of needs from different categories (see Figure 8).

	I RECOGNIZE	I DON'T RECOGNIZE
YOU RECOGNIZE	SATISFIED Traditional Standard Obvious Natural Routine	THANKFUL Perceptions Deductions Inferences Educated guesses Analogies
YOU DON'T RECOGNIZE	FULFILLED Secrets Dreams Aspirations Goals Insecurities	ENRICHED Mysteries Different Perspectives Misperceptions Misinterpretations

Figure 8. Classification of Feelings when Needs are Met

Meeting Service needs brings Satisfaction. Meeting Benevolence needs arouses Thankfulness. Needs met in Ministry evoke Fulfillment. Needs met in Therapy yield feelings of Enrichment. It is worthwhile noting that actions within the Service, Ministry, and Benevolence categories roughly correspond to the three dimensions of trustworthy behavior (Lewicki, 2003); thus, trust will build as the giver meets direct needs, acts in accordance with client motivations, and demonstrates caring by meeting needs initially unrecognized by the client. Knowing that the giver acts in accordance with a genuine interest in the other party's welfare sets the precedent for moral reciprocity for all future interaction—treating others, as you would like to be treated. This reciprocity is not in the form of gifts or concessions, but in dealing with fairness and an objective of mutual gain.

TRADEABLES CATEGORIZATION

We have already seen how the Johari window helps us to categorize the needs and the satisfaction of fulfilling a need. Now let's use that same tool to provide categories of Tradeables. Considering Tradeables as meeting unexpressed client or counterparty needs, they may either be hidden from you (Quadrant 3) or Unknown to the client (Quadrants 1 or 4). The traditional interpersonal communication model suggests improvement in communication effectiveness by widening the Arena area through use of active listening skills and giving and receiving feedback. This is true only if the information given and received is appropriate, relevant, and privileged. Without a bridge of trust through relationship, there may be: 1) reluctance to share; 2) exposure of superficial needs; or 3) exchange of deliberate misinformation.

Tradeables in the Service area lead to client Satisfaction. These needs are traditional, standard, obvious, natural, or routine. Mutual recognition of these needs is usually what brings parties to the table. This is the goal of most business transactions and negotiations. Directly meeting a need here outside of your primary reason for business interaction usually does not constitute a Tradeable so long as your deal is not consummated. Meeting or offering to meet these needs would be Trade-ins or Trade-offs. Meeting a need in the Service area before the deal can easily be construed as a bribe. After the deal, however, these needs are fertile ground for Tradeables, as they create leverage for future deals.

Indirectly meeting needs in Service, such as through a referral, would generally meet the Tradeables definition at any point in the business relationship. It is possible that Tradeables in the Service area may never exceed a Quintás level of one, a mere exchange of objects; thus, this is the least effective avenue for Tradeables.
If the need was initially unrecognized by the client, but you were able through a process of Revelation to expose and validate that need, you would generate feelings of Thankfulness in addition to the primary need for

Satisfaction. Thus, you achieved a Quintas level above one. Since knowledge of these needs was generated by imperfect means (perceptions, deductions, inferences, educated guesses, or analogies), the process of validation is crucial. Meeting a perceived need is ineffective if the client does not see it as, or is not fully convinced it is, a need. Validation actually transports the need out of the Blind area into the Arena area, but with it comes the feeling of Thankfulness. If a Service need was known to the client, but the client did not recognize you were able to meet that need, a Tradeable in the Service area will still lead to feelings of Thankfulness. Generally, all needs met in the Benevolence area qualify as Tradeables; however, the range of effectiveness can be widespread. We associate a nominal Quintás level of two with meeting Benevolence needs using Tradeables.

If the client has undisclosed or hidden needs that, through a relationship, can be exposed via active listening, it can be considered a Ministry. These needs can be secrets, dreams, aspirations, goals, and insecurities. As such, you are meeting deeper needs of the client that serve a greater purpose than those responsible for the encounter. These needs are not initially exposed, due to a lack of trust or feelings of reserve. These items can be deeply personal and emotional. The danger is exposure of needs that cannot be met; thus, training and a good referral system are paramount. The feelings generated by meeting needs initially in the Façade category are much stronger than those from other categories. Through disclosure and movement into Arena level, the client with these needs met feels Fulfilled and Satisfied. All needs met initially in the Ministry category should qualify as *Tradeables* and carry the greatest leverage while managing risk in the business relationship. We associate a nominal Quintas level of three to meeting needs of Ministry using *Tradeables*.

If needs are unknown to both parties, they could be mysteries, wrong perspectives, misperceptions, or misinterpretations. Finding and meeting these needs involves a process of Discovery. Since the needs were initially unknown and unrecognized, the client with these needs met feels Enriched and Satisfied. Depending on the recognition pathway of Discovery, the client could also be either Fulfilled or Thankful.

The level of significance of the need originally in the Unknown area can vary greatly. Needs met in Therapy should constitute *Tradeables*, yet this category carries the lowest frequency of success and greatest risk. Again, professional assistance may be required if exposed needs cannot be met directly. Still, we associate a Quintas level of four to successfully meeting Therapy needs using *Tradeables*.

EXERCISE PRUDENCE

The ability to generate *Tradeables* is directly related to a prudent person, as this active listener asks questions that explore the full range of needs of the other party. For the prudent, the ultimate goal of negotiation is to carefully observe the road to the objective, to learn that ups and downs are part of the experience. Being prudent is being aware that our conception of history, circular or linear vision, also allows us to understand the meaning that we are giving to the road of successful negotiation. He who is prudent integrates this vision into his research because he knows the importance and consequences of each conception.

As we saw earlier, in the matter of human relationships there is nothing "chemically perfect." Progress and setbacks, successes and frustrations, the ups and downs of each relationship are challenges that we encounter to find balance and transcendence. The prudent person is he who has the capacity to separate. Discernment comes from the verb *Krineo*, which means to separate the elements to bring to the negotiating table to give a sense of transcendance to the deal.

A discernment tool is precisely categorizing *Tradeables*, because it helps us to distinguish the immediate and pragmatic interest of a flawed negotiation and separate it from the root problem to help us focus on the transcendental benefit of the negotiation, both for the negotiator and for the receiver.

The exercise of prudence is, in itself, a challenge on a personal level. When man ceases to be prudent, he feels superior to God and the lack of humility blinds him. If we remember what happened with Babel's Tower, we see that the greatest obstacle to complete its construction was pride; believing that we can do it all without getting help from others disconnects us from others, and acting without the guidance of a transcendent sense makes us lose direction and enter into chaos.

The dialogue between Abraham and Yahveh about the salvation or destruction of Sodom and Gomorrah is a good example of how to apply prudence without losing the sense of transcendence.

Genesis 18:16-33

Abraham Pleads for Sodom
[16] *When the men got up to leave, they looked down toward Sodom, and Abraham walked along with them to see them on their way.*
[17] *Then the LORD said, "Shall I hide from Abraham what I am about to do?*
[18] *Abraham will surely become a great and powerful nation, and all nations on earth will be blessed through him.[a]*
[19] *For I have chosen him, so that he will direct his children and his household after him to keep the way of the LORD by doing what is right and just, so that the LORD will bring about for Abraham what he has promised him."*
[20] *Then the LORD said, "The outcry against Sodom and Gomorrah is so great and their sin so grievous*
[21] *that I will go down and see if what they have done is as bad as the outcry that has reached me. If not, I will know."*
[22] *The men turned away and went toward Sodom, but Abraham remained standing before the LORD.[b]*
[23] *Then Abraham approached him and said: "Will you sweep away the righteous with the wicked?*

²⁴ *What if there are fifty righteous people in the city? Will you really sweep it away and not spare[c] the place for the sake of the fifty righteous people in it?*
²⁵ *Far be it from you to do such a thing—to kill the righteous with the wicked, treating the righteous and the wicked alike. Far be it from you! Will not the Judge of all the earth do right?"*
²⁶ *The LORD said, "If I find fifty righteous people in the city of Sodom, I will spare the whole place for their sake."*
²⁷ *Then Abraham spoke up again: "Now that I have been so bold as to speak to the Lord, though I am nothing but dust and ashes,*
²⁸ *what if the number of the righteous is five less than fifty? Will you destroy the whole city for lack of five people?" "If I find forty-five there," he said, "I will not destroy it."*
²⁹ *Once again he spoke to him, "What if only forty are found there?" He said, "For the sake of forty, I will not do it."*
³⁰ *Then he said, "May the Lord not be angry, but let me speak. What if only thirty can be found there?" He answered, "I will not do it if I find thirty there."*
³¹ *Abraham said, "Now that I have been so bold as to speak to the Lord, what if only twenty can be found there?" He said, "For the sake of twenty, I will not destroy it."*
³² *Then he said, "May the Lord not be angry, but let me speak just once more. What if only ten can be found there?" He answered, "For the sake of ten, I will not destroy it."*
³³ *When the LORD had finished speaking with Abraham, he left, and Abraham returned home.*

Although Abraham seemed very "bold" for questioning Yahveh, what he is really doing is appealing to His kindness and His infinite wisdom, requesting that Yahveh, instead of turning to destruction, exercise discernment. Similarly, when talking about prudence we cannot stop thinking about discernment. It is necessary to discern not only before acting, but also before making a judgment that aspires to be founded. If we do not separate "righteous from sinners" we will derail any negotiation, whether personal or business. In other words, it is not enough to have clear principles; before making a judgment we must seek fundamentals.

People tend to select data and, based on our customs, upbringing, experiences and belief system, we constantly make inferences and act accordingly. We tend to act quickly. This is called the ladder of inference, where two people tend to quickly infer and develop fixed positions that are not understood unless a connection and dialogue between people is established.

I would call this an elevator of inferences, since at each encounter, we tend to infer many things about the actions and situations of others based on our own assumptions. It is not that inferring is a bad or evil thing, but taking actions based on the wrong inference will produce wrong behaviors and a lack of trust. Misunderstandings lead to conflictive situations without bases, and we would do better to make multiple inferences and try to test accuracy by asking questions, verifying proposing and affirming to the other side. Doing so could lead to better deals.

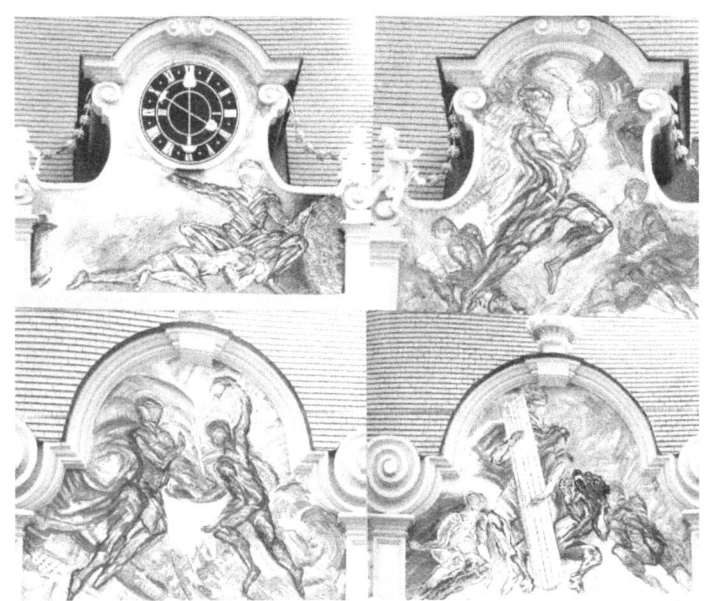

Discerning is knowing how to take the best path.
Fresco P. Bischof (1988/90)
The Four Cardinal Virtues in the Monastery of Melk, Austria

Two people quickly climb the ladder of inference and, anchored in its position without understanding each other, they leave much value in the negotiating table.

ASK BEFORE YOU REACT

On one occasion I traveled from Houston to Mexico and only had with me a carry-on suitcase of the appropriate size to bring on board, so it fit perfectly in the cabin of smaller aircraft in which I travel at least three times a month. I was the first to get on the plane and put my bag in the overhead compartment. With visible anger the flight attendant shouted at me, *"Nooo!"*

"Sorry, what is the problem?" I asked.

"Do not stow that suitcase there," the attendant responded.

In confusion, I asked, "This is not the first time I have brought a suitcase to the cabin. Has the regulation changed for carry-ons? When? Could you please explain?"

Illogic was the way the flight attendant was behaving; however, I did not want to get into an argument so I started to empty my suitcase, which contained all the electronics of my trip and my computer. I was preparing to empty the bag to give to the flight attendant, when I called my wife Marcela and told her in Spanish, "I can't believe that the flight attendant won't let me put the suitcase in the airplane compartment. It is the required size and it fits perfectly. I'll take a picture to send to the airline when I get back and demand an explanation for the return trip." At that time, the flight attendant returned "as a soul in torment," as we say in Mexico, that is, at full speed, and he started shouting in Spanish to me, "Do you know I can thrown you off the plane if I wanted? You can't take a picture of me."

He also threatened that he could sue me. And then he added, "This is not Mexico, sir." I was furious at his comment but I tried to justify it to myself and instead of counterattacking him, I decided to ask questions to clarify the situation. The airplane was almost at full capacity by this time. Next to me were two crewmen who were on vacation to Mexico and most of the passengers were Mexicans who spoke fluent English as well. I was in the first row of the plane and started talking loudly in English, turning back to connect with the group and so that everyone understood me. "You tell me that this is not Mexico? What do you mean? Would you explain? In addition, don't you work for a USA airline that has more flights and business in Mexico than the Mexican airlines? Isn't that right? Where are we going now? Mexico, right? What do you mean this is not Mexico? You know I'm also an American citizen? And why are you threatening that you could take me off the plane? I am a frequent flyer and this is the first time I can't bring the carryon on board. Would you explain why? And I wish to know your name."

At that time, he handed me the suitcase and told me that as he had already closed the flight, my suitcase could stay on the plane, but I could not put it into the compartment. He did not give me his name; in fact, he hid his name badge. Seated behind me there was a couple from Mexico, who I did not know. The husband turned and said, "Just put your bag up there; do not worry." I told him that this guy had treated me very badly and that I should not leave it at that.

As the flight attendant had quickly inferred that I was going to take a picture of him, not the suitcase, his reaction was threatening to have me removed from the plane. I, seeking not to worsen the situation, wanted to ask questions in order to reach an agreement. We arrived to Mexico and I was curious to know from other passengers what they thought about my behavior, in order to study and improve. The day after my arrival into Mexico, at the event where I had been invited as the Keynote speaker, personalities such as the secretary of state of education and university officials were present. Before I started my talk, I heard that they were waiting for a certain person named "Pancho" to start the program. Pancho, the chairman of the organization, finally arrived and approached me to invite me to start. To both our surprise, Pancho was the person who was sitting behind me on the airplane, the one who had told me not to worry and just to put my suitcase in the overhead compartment. When we were at the event, we became fast friends after my talk. At the reception, Pancho told me without me asking him, "You were fantastic on the airplane! I understand now why you are the expert in negotiation; you handled yourself very well on the plane. "

From this example we can learn several lessons. First, the flight attendant inferred that I was going to take a picture of him and he acted in accordance with his inference. On the contrary, I didn't want to make any inference at any time about what he might have meant by his statement "This is not Mexico." Inferring one meaning is limiting; having done so, I would put myself quickly on one extreme position and the flight attendant on the other extreme, and this could have led to a fight. In a negotiation, inferring and acting upon that inference may not lead to agreement and, even worse, may lead us to position ourselves in extremes that can be polarized. Another lesson learned is that we are all interrelated. My bad behavior toward the flight attendant could have affected my future actions and vice versa. If, for example, I had chosen to compete and attack the flight attendant in an arrogant manner, it could have created distrust in my negotiating skills with Pancho when he learned that I was the expert in conflict management and negotiation Speaker.

Each time I go out on a business trip, I carry my garment bag as part of my hand luggage on the plane. The first thing I do when getting on the plane, which is almost a habit, is to ask if they can hang my clothes in the small closet. One day, while climbing the stairs of the airplane, I realized that a crew member was giving me a "NO" signal with his body language, shaking his head from left to right. Why was he saying no? Perhaps he had a tic or a problem, I concluded. While finishing up the stairs, I kept thinking and I convinced myself that the "NO" of the flight attendant was not directed at me. He had not even opened his mouth. My first approach to the crew member was not asking him to hang my garment bag; instead I asked him, "Everything okay? You seem distressed."

"Yes, I am surprised. I just arrived from a flight and now I just learned I have to cover this new shift as well."

"Do not worry," I said, "this will be a great flight and we will enjoy ourselves."

"Can I help you with your garment bag?" he asked.

"That's very kind," I smiled. "Thank you very much."

What is the moral of the story? When we avoid making judgments based on inferences, we can better understand the other party. If, for a moment, we stop being selfish, thinking only of our need, and satisfy the other, simply asking if everything is okay, we can reach more robust negotiation solutions for both parties. We believe that it is not wrong to infer, but rather one should engage in several inferences and ask before making judgments, to keep open the path of agreement and avoid creating barriers to that end.

Today "quick action" is rewarded often; success is associated with who is the fastest to achieve the goal, but often we can learn that what is gained today may be lost tomorrow. The good news is that we can combine the two speeds, slow to discern and agile to act. In discernment the negotiator should take all the time necessary, but the execution of the previously discerned action must be quick.

PRUDENCE AND IMPRUDENCE

The terms prudence and discernment are very close concepts. The word 'discern' itself suggests exploring two or more possibilities and seeing clearly the best option. Everyone is able to discern consciously and freely discover alternatives to make a good decision. What elements would be enough to choose well? St. Thomas Aquinas would say, "To achieve a good decision, prudence is required." One of the preconditions of every human is making choices; this is why everyone's homework is to exercise prudence.

The characteristic of a conscious, responsible and free person, able to face reality in a lucid way, is prudential discernment. Negotiation cannot become imprudent, reactive or impulsive, responding to blind instinct or giving in to the pressure exerted by the passions or the exercise of power. But even a wise king like King Solomon may fail to make effective use of *Tradeables*. The Hebrew Scriptures narrate that King Solomon sent an unsolicited present to the Phoenician king Hiram to show his pleasure after twenty years of work on the construction of the temple and palace. The gift consisted of twenty cities around Galilee. When King Hiram went to inspect his gift, he did not seem so pleased and asked to Solomon, "What kind of towns have you given me, my brother?" Although the letter was a negative report, by calling Solomon "my brother" in the same sentence, King Hiram focused criticism on the gift and not on the relationship itself. As Harvard scholars say, you have to separate the problem from the person; be hard on the problem and soft on the person. We do not have to track the disposition of these towns; we know they did not enjoy any particular brightness. What is clear from the response of King Hiram is that the King Solomon's use of *Tradeables* was not very effective.

Effective use of *Tradeables* involves using prudence and discernment to meet those customer needs that are not related to the matter of business. These towns apparently did not meet any need, hidden or exposed, of King Hiram—a lesson for all those eager to practice *Tradeables* in negotiations. A responsible negotiator who has overcome the stage of instincts, discerns as a reflective activity full-time, because it allows him to identify problems during the negotiation process and transform them into opportunities, always in tune with truth and justice.

Another way to feed prudence is to recognize when we are being imprudent. To do so, the story of the four horses and the lion is very illustrative.

Once there were four horses so powerful and united that there was no force or energy in the universe that could undo the connection between them.

One day a lion visited the four horses. The lion began to whisper to each horse that besides being more intelligent than the others he was also better than the others. The horses were so close that the lion could not beat them, until the lion had an idea: the lion told one horse that the other three had stolen from his harvest.

Thus, the lion continued putting weeds after weeds, year after year, until the day came when the horses were destroyed by each other's envy, hatred, resentment, anger and ego, until they faded away and came close to extinction.

Unusual vase topped by four horses Museum of Cycladic Art, Athens, Greece.

Who are the four horses? The company, employees, families, and community. Who is the lion? It is all that separates us from the transcendental sense of a negotiation and that makes us behave imprudently. Don't forget that the goal of the negotiation, regardless of the context, is going to be achieved in the process itself. We can achieve success not only by reaching the end goal but also by choosing the right route to accomplish that negotiation goal.

This requires perseverance, regularity, maintaining a real tension, and being aware that almost always we move forward in a spiral way with progress and setbacks and not necessarily in a linear progression. But on the whole, we move chasing a goal that goes beyond what we provide when we enter the negotiation. You may be imprudent by being inconsistent. This is one of the diseases of our society; the anxiety for immediate results often prevents a negotiation from resulting in a firm agreement.

We have to be very self-critical in our interaction, as there is a kind of prudence that we can consider harmful, as it is a false virtue. The ancients called it *Astutia* and is a kind of simulation that a person incorporates into their behavior when they are only attracted by the value of tactical or strategic negotiations.

This attitude is the breeding ground for mistrust and intrigue, cancers of any relationship. Facing the *Astutia*, categorizing *Tradeables* is a good antidote, allowing us to recognize harmful inertia from the first encounter.

It is true that you can get to a right end by false and crooked ways. How often this happens in the "art of negotiation"! And how much energy is wasted on the road and how much distrust and suspicion engendered! The proper sense of the prudent is that not only is it aligned to the truth, but also the path leading to it.

Lion's head, Phoenician culture, V and IV centuries B.C., San Antioco, Sardinia. Museum of ancient sculpture, Giovanni Barrocco.

We need to recognize the pseudo-prudences: even though these allow us to play smart, they are born of greed or pleonetia, Greek term which refers to the insatiable desire to possess and accumulate, and this will generate a growing frustration.

Selfish interests must be silenced in any negotiation process. The lack of authenticity and transparency, hiding places, tricks and disloyalty pollute the relationship; we become miserly. "Loving a son," says a Spanish proverb, "is not to force him to live with our truths, but help him so he can live without our lies." When we allow ourselves to be driven by negative behaviors, we fall into a kind of narcissism because we only look at ourselves, ignoring the truth of real things. Whoever acts in terms of ambitions and selfish interests can be neither fair nor brave nor moderate, much less prudent.

In all countries (not only in Latin America but also in some European countries) the credibility of the political class is questioned. The reason is clear: after falling into scandalous levels of selfishness they are betraying the commitments made to the citizens who elected them. In theory, their personal interests should be neutralized in order to achieve the public good. And the first thing we should demand from a politician is to practice the virtue of justice and not the false virtue of *Astutia*.

All this leads us to another key and fundamental concept in our thinking. Prudence, essentially ordered to the means and not the end, presupposes the moral law that culture has imprinted on us from the Judeo-Christian worldview. One of the sources of this law is the Ten Commandments; it suffices to follow them to conduct ourselves with prudence and give transcendance to negotiation. Negotiations are not manipulations that can be determined in advance; in fact, they can be considered moral actions that lead the subject to self-realization. The more moral an action is, the more "righteous" is the negotiation process and the more the person feels self-realization, regardless of where this person is coming from. As the poet Paul Claudet says, prudence "is the patient light that shines on us not in the future, but in the immediate future."

To educate ourselves in the art of prudence is to implement the objective assessment of the specific situation in which an action takes place, as well as the power to transform this concept of reality into a personal decision.

The patient light that enlightens us. Puerto Vallarta, Mexico

REFLECTION EXERCISE

HOW PRUDENT ARE YOU?

1. Do you have inner peace?
2. Can you identify what controls your willpower?
3. Are you able to recognize the appropriate moment to make a move in a negotiation?
4. Do you know which ideas and actions are in harmony with your thoughts and feelings?
5. Do you have clear directionality and a sense of where you're going?
6. Are you able to see the beginning, middle and end of a negotiation process?
7. Are you aware of your inconsistencies or weaknesses in your thought processes and willpower in your negotiation with the counterparty?
8. In addition to examining the end result of the DEAL, do you also know whether the outcomes of the negotiation are transcendental for you or the counterparty?
9. Do you know how to identify the negotiation process critical path?
10. Do you challenge the result and the negotiation process with the appropriate ethical or regulatory framework?

% of Prudence in Dealing = Number YES/10*100 =_____%

CHAPTER III
JUSTICE

For those who do not believe in a transcendent entity, justice is relative; for those that do, justice is absolute. Vatican Museum Photo: Habib Chamoun-Farah.

WHAT DO WE UNDERSTAND BY JUSTICE?

There is a dilemma that every human being faces at least once in life: to be fair or unfair. For those who do not believe in a transcendent entity, justice is relative; for those who do, justice is absolute. After all, this situation is like the negotiator dilemma. Should I collaborate or should I compete? Am I fair or am I unfair?

In Mexico there are two cities in the same bay, Puerto Vallarta and Nuevo Vallarta, each in two different states of the Mexican federation, Jalisco and Nayarit, respectively. The dilemma hoteliers in both cities face is whether they compete or collaborate with each other. In a project conducted with the support of the newspaper *Vallarta Opina*, we developed an exercise in game theory with the different stakeholders in both cities: authorities, hoteliers, opinion leaders, and so on. The game revealed the dilemma of competing to attract tourists or collaborating to generate profits to stay in the area and use the resources of the federation to be promoted as a single destination instead of two, to avoid confusing tourists and discouraging them from visiting both places. After participating in the exercise the interested stakeholders began promoting the area as a single destination with two options. While both cities continue to compete to drive up standards and improve the quality of service, they are now collaborating as well so that money is not left on the negotiation table for promoting both of the cities.

This exercise reminds us that neighbors or not, we are interrelated in many ways, so we could have more common interests than we imagined. If we stop only thinking about our self-interest for a moment, we will achieve more profits in the long run. The above story introduces us to what we mean by justice in the framework of a transcendental negotiation. The classical authors define justice as a moral virtue that consists of the constant and firm will to give to God, like in the time of the Phoenicians, and to others what is right. Justice in the negotiation involves respecting the rights of each party. When the rights of any of the negotiation actors are not respected or when a human relationship is not established to ensure harmony or promote fairness, respect or common good, a negotiation process vitiates, contrary to the type of relationship established when we involve the *Tradeables*. The usual righteous thoughts and behavior in relation to others are essential, since the negotiation process is contaminated by acting according to inferences. Behaving under the inertia of prejudice can ruin the successful completion of negotiations.

Justice as a human virtue ultimately lies in an inner motivational force, and not so much in a will for power. This means that in real negotiation, to be fair, you do not need the *potestas* (power) as much as the *autoritas* (authority). The philosopher Giovanni Sartori says those in authority are in a position to enforce, confirm or sanction a course of action or thought. Power is not the same as authority.

I can have more power in negotiations under my financial capacity, but no authority for lack of moral principles. What makes me just in negotiation is not having power but above all not lacking authority. On the other hand, justice also needs generosity in negotiating, as evidenced by the use of *Tradeables*, i.e., it doesn't mean that you will get a fair negotiation with mere restitution (an exchange of haggling), but justice cries for an added delivery beyond the win-win. That extra is part of the generosity that founded Christianity in Western culture and remains a reference of development. The blood of the martyrs was the seed of a new civilization, as well as the dedication of the Benedictine monks through culture, arts and religion (*Tradeables*) that spread across Europe, overcoming injustices that came from pagan models distant from the Judeo-Christian worldview. Another aspect that will rescue justice is the need to integrate a great deal of understanding; it is important to get in the other's shoes to better understand their situation. In a negotiation, empathy (Greek *pathos, pathia em:* suffer with) is given to the extent that the other feels their needs are understood. An optimal degree of understanding involves not only stay at the level of the intellect, but also attending to the emotional dimension, i.e., the operational mechanisms of emotion that extend or reduce the field of understanding. A father and a mother understand the child because they love him, more so than they love him because they understand him. In a negotiation, the other party is not indifferent. This is not to say that you have to love the other party, but if knowledge is based on a connection that is not purely rational but also emotional and volitional, the more empathy is created, the more solid will be the relationship underlying the negotiation process. This is precisely the effect of *Tradeables*.

A variant of justice is called social justice. Do not forget that the development of economic activities is designed to meet the needs of human beings, that is, economic life is not meant solely to multiply the production or increase the power, but it is at the service of people and community. When we talk about social justice we are talking about rights, including the fundamental right of work, because the person develops at work part of the capabilities inscribed in his very nature. As the book of Thessalonians says, "If anyone will not work, let him not eat." Work is for man, not man for work. This is an application of the virtue of justice. Similarly, we can say that negotiation is for man and not man for negotiation. Different interests, often opposed to one another, often affect business economic life from which social conflict is explained. Therefore, it is necessary to strive to reduce this conflict through negotiation, so that the rights and duties of each party are respected: those responsible, entrepreneurs and representatives of workers and public authorities.

The issue of social justice means overcoming institutional, legal and political gaps, while ensuring individual freedom, the right to private property, a stable currency and efficient public service.

Social justice urges the State to monitor and prosecute the exercise of human rights in the economic sector, forgetting that the first responsibility is not that of the State but of every individual, group and association in which society is structured. This is called "principle of subsidiarity," and it is that by which one assumes the responsibilities that do not have to take place at the State level. In the context of social justice it is impossible to ignore solidarity. You cannot have a fair negotiation with inequality of resources and economic means. Because inequality of resources and economic means generates an abyss, it is an asymmetrical relationship that makes us easily fall into the law of the strongest over the weakest. For example, if between two golfers, one has the antiquated and the other state–of-the art equipment; even if the first player is more skillful he may lose effectiveness due to the lack of resources and technology.

In ancient civilizations, the means for war were not so asymmetric, but that does not mean that one party was more powerful than the other. If any army was winning it was because of strategy rather than resources. The good negotiator is not the one that handles more economic resources, but the one with better negotiation skills or operational strategies. If the negotiation is asymmetric it is unfair. A good negotiator prefers not to enter the game. For example, poker players have the same number of cards, which means that, at least in principle, the game is fair and just. Therefore, it is a duty of justice that we work to achieve a level of equal conditions.

Technology equipment and support to reach a negotiation with greater efficiency, as in the case of golfers. Photo: Habib Chamoun-Farah.

INJUSTICE

Corruption of justice has two causes, according to St. Thomas Aquinas: "the false wisdom of the wise and the clairvoyance of the powerful." One example of false prudence is the case of the towns that King Solomon gave to King Hiram of Phoenicia; another is the case of Samson. We are interested in working with this thought of St. Thomas because it has a scope almost prophetic in our societies where, "under the guise of good," some hide aggressiveness and violent transgression of the moral law, as the "shark" that feeds on the win-win-win at the expense of whatever it takes. Both human vulnerability and incompetence are revealed in something as profane and at the same time moral as the negotiation.

Hence we have to make justice a *habitus* (a constant will not accepting alternation in its development) to give each one his own right.

A person who steals from another instead of giving her what she owes has violated and disfigures herself. It is she who loses and self-destructs. In any negotiation, lying, theft, extortion, and other behaviors that depersonalize the subject are stones that sooner or later fall on their own roof. In the long run, the evil experienced by the offender is worse than the damage suffered by the victim. Plato says in the dialogue Gorgias that "the height of ignominy is not to be slapped, nor in running into the hands of a robber or murderer (...) To commit an injustice on my person reports more damage to the one responsible for the act than to myself, despite being its victim." So even if it is more traumatic, sometimes it's better to be on the side of the one suffering theft and extortion from the "Shark" than being to be incapable of negotiating humanely. And here we return to our first pillar: prudence. What characterizes justice regarding prudence is that Justice's task is to generate order to the "I" in everything that has to do with a "you." Prudence, however, is dedicated to perfecting the "I" advising what suits oneself. By integrating these two virtues, we see why it is so important to take seriously the other in the negotiation, acknowledge his integrity as a person and not as a mere instrument to be used or competitor who has to be annihilated or defeated. Justice shows that the other is someone who is not me but, like me, the other is entitled to his rights. A person is just to the extent which he recognizes the otherness of the other and tries to give him what he deserves. That is to act as one should. However, within the duty there is a hierarchy or graduation of differences. For example, if in the framework of the business deal I am committed to someone at a purchase price, I must meet my agreement strictly; it is useless if I invite him to eat as an act of kindness if I do not comply with the agreement.

I am bound more tightly to not deceive that person than to invite him to dinner at the best restaurant. Going further still, we can say that the other is not reached or touched by what I believe, think, feel or want about him, but what I do and how I do it. The deal with the other has to transcend my subjective or my mood appreciations. In a negotiation, only through actions can one restore or give to the other what it is his.

One can commit an act of injustice without being unjust. Often in negotiation injustices are committed in the formal and material, and that does not make us directly unjust beings. Take the example of a man who has a company whose technology is obsolete. He wants to act justly to keep the business afloat and workers employed. Moreover, another man wants to purchase that company to reengineer it, but this would involve firing plant workers. In the immediate future, the employer would be acting with justice and the buyer would be committing an injustice. If you look long term, workers would remain stagnant for longer, would probably lose the opportunity to get a job where they can be trained, and the owner would not be able to collect the fruit of years of effort. Selling the company is not so unfair when we go beyond the immediate. We could reason it out in reverse: it does not need to be first right to do "what is right." It is a paradoxical reality. The generation of a righteous act is required by the mere fact that you have to do it in the order of law, and not because the realizing of that something has to come from the act of justice.

It is for this reason that respect for the regulatory framework in which a negotiation develops is so important and decisive. I can find people with many shortcomings in what is referred to as the habit of justice, but these people perform just acts through a series of rules that must be respected, as in the case of the unjust people who have been saved for justice. An emblematic case is the biblical people of Israel, who escaped and entered the Promised Land to respect a code. Those who were behind the idols were not spared.

JUSTICE ON A LARGE SCALE

[1]But the souls of the just are in the hand of God, and the torment of death shall not touch them.[2] In the sight of the unwise they seemed to die: and their departure was taken for misery:[3] And their going away from us, for utter destruction: but they are in peace.[4] And though in the sight of men they suffered torments, their hope is full of immortality.[5] Afflicted in few things, in many they shall be well rewarded: because God hath tried them, and found them worthy of himself.[6] As gold in the furnace he hath proved them, and as a victim of a holocaust he hath received them, and in time there shall be

respect had to them.[7] The just shall shine, and shall run to and fro like sparks among the reeds.

Wisdom 3 (1-7)

Once I was invited as a speaker by a Mexican businessman who lives in southern Mexico; after I met him it changed my perception of the typical Mexican businessman whose self-interest is more important than the common interest. His business is a series of bakeries accessible to the masses at bus stops, and his market niche is the lowest socio-economic stratus of the population in the region. I was struck by the human quality and sincerity of this man. Since then, I ask participants in my courses how many of them know this kind of entrepreneur, small or medium. All raise their hands. Then I ask how many of those entrepreneurs who you know give scholarships to the children of their employees in the most prestigious universities in the country if their children get good grades? Only one of 50 participants raises his hand.

Finally, I wonder how many of these entrepreneurs, if they find that the children of their employees have gotten into gangs, personally try to get them out of trouble. Nobody answers. I have asked this question to more than two thousand young fortunates. Most of them are sons of entrepreneurs, and the situation is repeated. It is for this reason that this southern businessman is unique: he dares to risk for others; he is sincere with himself and with others.

I am fortunate to have met a dozen Mexican businessmen who follow these steps, and I think there must be many more, but they are "invisible to the eye." Thanks to those entrepreneurs interested in the common good above their own good, Mexico and the world are moving ahead. However, these entrepreneurs do not make much noise, and what sells to the media is noise. The Book of Sirach has a great teaching about this:

> [14] *My* children, keep discipline in peace: For wisdom that is hid, and a treasure *that is* not seen, What profit *is* in *them* both? [15] *A man that hideth his foolishness* is *better Than a man that hideth his wisdom.* (Sirach 41: 14-15).

Reflect. What kind of entrepreneur do you want to be, one who makes noise or one who leaves a positive mark on his life and the lives of others. It is our choice to be or not to be socially responsible.

When one acts justly, it is favoring the effectiveness of good. By its very nature, the good calls to operate out, communicate, radiate. For example, the Phoenicians invented the alphabet to communicate better with their people, but also shared it with other people. The smart thing is to use our own goodness not only for ourselves but for others. Similarly to what happens with evil, the clumsiest way to be wrong is to let our meanness extend its effects not only to oneself but also to our friends. As St. Thomas says, justice lies in the noblest part of the soul; it reaches its true wealth not only when you see the truth, but when it converts into action. Thus, the more effective a good is, the farther it radiates goodness.

What makes a particular State more just than another? Why are the big multinationals wary of those States where the level of corruption is beyond the limits of a society that is proudly called democratic? There is justice in a State when everyone's conscience is clear that the ultimate effect of a crime is not so much associated with the losses that carry the transgression, but more so with the threat to the order and disruption of coexistence.

To understand how this system works on a larger scale, consider three fundamental relationships that involve three forms of justice:

1. Commutative justice, which is what articulates the relationship between individuals.
2. Distributive justice, which articulates the relationship between the community and the individuals who are part of it.
3. The legal or general justice, which regulates and articulates the relationship of individuals to the social whole.

The health of a country, in terms of justice, is measured based on these three parameters. When these fundamental relationships are not given, there is no hope. The doctor in theology Felix Palazzi[6] says that hope, rather than a state of mind or the projection of our good wishes, is the engine of justice:

Hope motivates us to seek and build justice, the justice which obviously is not directly comparable to our legal system, that is, justice has its expression in a legal code and in its institutions, but it is much more than its legal expression, because its purpose is really to protect the difference and ensure that it exists. That is why only hope creates justice and within the injustice our hope grows, for hope is strengthened when hosting the hope of others. Hope moves us to participation and transformation of reality.

Many people believe that it is a utopian desire to think that there can be just political structures, particularly in some countries of Latin America, Eastern Europe, Asia or Africa. But the advance of history is due to the great utopias. Negotiating with ethics and values is utopian? We think it is not. In fact, we believe establishing relations on a fair basis gives us hope. But today more than ever we have to face the challenge of educating and training ethical people to become transcendental negotiators. Without education in values, it is not that we are not going to be good negotiators, it is that there will not be people with whom to negotiate. An infallible principle underlying any negotiations says that you have to go a little beyond what is considered fair, because only the righteous are willing to do more than they should.

It is naive to think that social, economic and political structures achieve the desired order by the single action of justice. Therefore, in the course of a negotiation, as in life itself, debts, obligations or duties are given that exclude the possibility of satisfaction or proportional

[6] http://www.teologiahoy.com/esperanza-y-justicia/

payment—so much so that a person who seriously strives to be fair by giving each one what he needs will still experience the feeling of "falling short." This feeling of inadequacy, perhaps motivated by the hope of building a better world, is what leads us to try to exceed the right. Perhaps this is the reason why people in advanced societies increasingly feel the need to develop a volunteer or charitable activity to extinguish this kind of anguish usually experienced by the insatiable consumer of false securities that ends up leaving him empty.

Companies that have developed in recent years the so-called social responsibility have also been affected by this feeling, increasingly growing and consolidating. Sometimes entrepreneurs think they should do great projects when it would be sufficient to simply transform their negotiations in the space of justice.

Sincerity, for example, is a form of justice and social responsibility, as in the experience of a negotiation process, we realize that there are benefits that will never be susceptible to coercion, but are obligatory, like someone telling the truth.

Gratitude is another form of justice. It's not just a polite formality or having good education. Psalm 4, also known as the night prayer, gives us a transcendent vision of a sense of gratitude. "Being grateful for favors received leads us to ask again. This request will be confident. The trust will attract peace and joy in the midst of difficulties." We understand this passage as follows: who asks God from the deficiency does not see the gifts he has received from day to day; who appreciates every night by his experiences is placed in a position of abundance, he realizes the possibilities and he is able to see opportunities for others. From there you can be fair, because knowing your options and those of others, you will give to everyone according to his work.

Gratitude is important because we close the circle of giving and receiving; a virtuous circle is more likely to generate wealth.

The Phoenicians are a great example. In the cities where they had ports and thriving businesses, they built temples of great beauty to thank their gods for the gifts they received. Read what one king says in this votive inscription dedicated to Ba'alat from Byblos:

> *I am Yehawmilk, king of Byblos, the son of Yeharba'al the grandson of son of Yeharbaal, the grandson of Urimilk, king of Byblos, whom the mistress, the Lady of Byblos, made king over Byblos... I have been calling my mistress, the Lady of Byblos, [and she heard my voice]. Therefore, I have made for my mistress, the Lady of Byblos, this altar of bronze which is in this [courtyard], and this <u>engraved object</u> of gold which is in front of this inscription of mine, with the bird(?) of gold that is set in a (<u>semiprecious</u>) stone, which is upon this <u>engraved object</u> of gold, and this portico with its columns and the [capitals] which are upon them, and its roof: I Yehawmilk, king of Byblos, as I called my mistress, the Lady of Byblos, and she heard my voice*

and treated me kindly. May the Lady of Byblos bless and preserve Yehawmilk, king of Byblos, and prolong his days and years in Byblos, for he is a righteous king. And may [the mistress,]the Lady of Byblos, give [him] favor in the eyes of the gods and in the eyes of the people of this country and (that he be)pleased with the people of this country. [Whoever you are,] ruler and (ordinary) man, who might [continue] to do work on this altar and this engraved work of gold and this portico, my name, Yehawmilk, king of Byblos [you should put with] yours upon that work, and if you do not put my name with yours, or if you [remove] this ... upon this place and ... [may] the mistress, the Lady of Byblos, [destroy] that man and his seed before all the gods of Byblos. (The Stele of Yehawmilk of Byblos (5th century BC): ANET 502)

QUICK TEST

On a Scale from 1 to 10...

Are you grateful?

Do you consider life a jail?

Are you happy?

Why are so many people so ungrateful? When people are not grateful they feel they deserve things and they do not see the need to give thanks. Ingratitude is, as in the negotiation process, similar to not giving feedback, which is essential to have an effective communication flow and prevent creating assumptions or inferences.

Generosity, liberality and affability (affabilitas, as St. Thomas Aquinas calls) are forms of justice and enhance the humanity of an "I" that is put into play before a "you", the one that has the same impulse of truth, good and beauty. When all of the above is lacking, the joy (*delectabiten*) is also missing. Just as a truly authentic human life is impossible without the truth, so it is when there is no joy.

Mercy is a principle that we can integrate when we are facing negotiating dilemmas. John Paul II, great exponent of social thought in the twentieth century, claimed that there would be no true justice without mercy. Mercy is exercised on large and small scales, for example, when the debt is forgiven to poor countries or to students who after graduating don't get jobs. However, sometimes there is a calculating desire that hides behind "doing the right thing," an effort that can become inhuman. Debt forgiveness is an act of mercy not because the other deserves it, but because by doing so, a plus is given, that extra that drives the righteous to do more than what is right. H. Gollwitzer, when recounting the memories of his captivity, recalled how veteran prisoners could not tolerate that ill comrades receive an equal portion of food which was not corresponding to their effective participation. "Given our appeal to their compassion and camaraderie they did not show the greater understanding that we did by facing this inexorable way to calculate what is owed – a calculation by the way, on which the entire life of the Soviet Union system is mounted."

The teachings of classical philosophers of Christianity[7] remind us that mercy without justice is the mother of dissolution, but justice without mercy is cruelty.

Another learning that leaves the exercise of justice is that of integrity. A negotiator without integrity cannot create a negotiation with a solid and lasting foundation. Carlos Maria Moreno Perez says, "By integrity I mean the set of standards of moral and intellectual honesty on which the conduct of a person is based. Without integrity we betray ourselves, we betray others and reduce the value of everything we started"(2001). Moreno Perez adds that without justice other virtues (prudence, discernment and temperance) will serve very little purpose.

People of a company must clearly see that the leader is right in his way of doing things. If justice is present from the top, leadership gains credibility with their subordinates. When arbitrariness, arrogance or simple lack of criteria are present in the conduct of the management, the possibility of conducting ethical leadership is lost.

I am convinced that in the coming years rigorous scholars will appear on the importance of virtues in managerial work. The review of classics like Aristotle, along with the daily pulse of managerial work in

---

[7] Josef Pieper mentioned in the fundamental virtues, Editions RIALP S.A., Madrid, 2003, p 172.

individual companies, undoubtedly will provide a greater depth in the direction of companies. It's time to take another step toward a direction focused on values and leadership based on virtues. In this regard, Juan Antonio Pérez-López writes these very wise words in his book *Leadership and Ethics in Business Management*:

> *When a businessman is unable to move his people other than through economic incentives, it is as bad professionally as the medical professional who is incapable of anything other than attacking the symptoms that the patient says he has. When he is able to move people through the work he offers and the professional learning he provides, it is now on another professional level; he is no longer just a strategist but an executive. When he is able to bring subordinates to discover the value and meaning of what they are doing, then and only then, is he a leader.*

A person who is not just with herself and with others is far from being a person with integrity. This book examines the subject of transcendental negotiation, studying in depth the virtues as pillars of a leader with ethics and integrity. The term *Tradeables*, from which we can extract the words DEAL and *trabes*, makes a lot more sense now. *Tradeables* comprises the basis of integrity and fairness necessary in any negotiation.

REFLECTION EXERCISE

HOW JUST AM I?

1. Do I notice much difference between reality and my expectations?
2. Does the truth play a very important role in my negotiation process?
3. Am I fair-minded when giving?
4. Is my style more integrative than distributive?
5. Do I care about justice in both the long term and the short term?
6. Do my negotiations contribute to establishing a more just order in life?
7. Is there a high level of social responsibility in my negotiation process?
8. Do I identify justice in my negotiations with the terms Equality, Dignity and Equity?
9. Will my decision regarding the community be a positive influence?
10. Is moral responsibility a factor in the course of my negotiating?

% of Justice - number of YES / 10 * 100 = _____ %

CHAPTER IV
FORTITUDE

Fortitude is the moral virtue that gives us, in the midst of difficulties, firmness and confidence to continue on the path of good. Joan of Arc, icon of strength. Church Trinita dei Monti, Rome, Italy

TO UNDERSTAND FORTITUDE

D brothers were maintenance providers for Company A, owner of a huge amusement park. For many years, the brothers gave maintenance to the rides in the park, until one day the amusement park management was changed. Newcomers requested the D brothers submit a quotation to include maintenance, equipment replacement and painting of the whole amusement park complex. After they had presented the best service proposal, the new administration called the brothers to come and discuss it. Confidentially the amusement park executives asked the D brothers to triple the quoted dollar amount but only charge once and deliver the difference in money to the amusement park management. They also asked the D brothers not to do in-depth work, but only to paint the rides and fail to effectively change parts or equipment needed. In other words, they put on the negotiating table the possibility of improving the profit with only a third of the work. The D brothers were in a dilemma. If they accepted and agreed to do less work for the same amount of money and gave two thirds of their income to the amusement park management, the risk of accepting this unethical proposal would be very high; if the D brothers did not accept, they would instantly be bankrupt when they stopped receiving income from their main customer, the amusement park.

What would you have done? I have asked this question to young students and graduate students, and many answered that they would have taken the job. The fortitude to say NO in a negotiation and end up with nothing the next day requires knowing how to discern between good and evil and have an unprecedented temperance. D brothers are a great example of how to be an excellent negotiator, because they decided to say no to their client, although bankruptcy was knocking on their door. Upon rejecting the offer of their main customer, the brothers wrote a registered letter stating the reasons why they did not accept the job. One reason was that they were well aware of a repair job that needed to be done and if was not executed it would become a latent risk. Moreover, for them it was inadmissible to lose their dignity for a job, and eventually they could lose both their work and their dignity.

Months after the D brothers rejected the agreement, a serious accident occurred in the amusement park that left several kids wounded and dead. The park tried to sue the D brothers without success. Fortunately, they had delivered a letter rejecting the proposal and explaining that they did not accept work unless they undertook repairs in depth, and they had recommended changing a series of mechanisms. They also mentioned in the letter the risk of not making the changes. In addition they specified that the amusement park had not accepted the measures suggested by the D brothers. This is why the lawsuit from the park did not proceed. To date, the family business continues to thrive with the same good reputation. What is the moral of this story? Definitely, temperance, discernment and fortitude are especially important features of the transcendent negotiator.

Fortitude, as we understand it here, is the moral virtue that through difficulties gives us the strength and confidence to continue on the path of good. It helps us resist temptations and to overcome moral obstacles. This virtue enables us to overcome fear and deal with the evidence or give in or sacrifice when necessary to defend a just cause. In our society, unfortunately marked by a radical liberalism, the original concept of a strong person is lost and tends to be confused with arrogance or authoritarian exercise of power. We are interested in stressing its original meaning. Why you have to be strong, and against whom? To be humble is to be strong?

St. Augustine said that the fort is "an undeniable witness" of the existence of evil. And that metaphysical condition helps us understand that in any human activity, the inertia of evil runs acts transversely. St. Thomas takes up the theme of the metaphysics of evil[8] and adds that this is not an essence or nature, nor a form nor self: evil is an absence of being, not a mere absence or denial, but deprivation of the good that should exist in one thing. Jacques Maritain[9] explains with impressive simplicity in a lecture in 1944:

---

[8] Speaking of metaphysics, we refer to one of the fundamental parts of philosophy that is responsible for studying "Being" and focuses attention on anything that transcends the merely physical.

[9] Jacques Maritain, "St. Thomas Aquinas and the problem of evil," lecture at Marquette University, Milwaukee, USA, 1944.

Evil does exist in things; it is terribly present in them. Evil is real, it actually exists like a wound or mutilation of the being; evil is there in all reality whenever a thing—which, insofar as it is, and has being, is good—is deprived of some being or some good it should have. Thus, evil exists in good, that is, the bearer of evil is good, insofar as it is being. And evil works through good, since evil, being in itself a privation or non-being, has no causality of its own. Evil is therefore efficacious not by itself but through the good it wounds and preys upon as a parasite, efficacious through a good that is wanting or deflected, and whose action is to that extent vitiated. What is thus the power of evil? It is the very power of the good that evil wounds and preys upon.

Any negotiation is somehow threatened by an evil that goes beyond the level of consciousness of the participants themselves. In our societies, evil[7] tends to become banal; it is not considered as dangerous as not to negotiate with it. "Everyone has his price" is one of the phrases that reveal its presence. But with the multiplicity of its forms and its multifaceted dimension, it cannot be negotiated with.

TURNING VULNERABILITY INTO FORTITUDE

In the attacks in November 2015 in the city of Paris, a journalist for 24 years, Antoine Leiris, lost his wife, the mother of his young son. In an act that breaks with the inertia of revenge that has made many people react negatively, Leiris published on his Facebook wall a moving letter from which we extract some excerpts:

On Friday night you stole the life of an exceptional human being, the love of my life, the mother of my child. But you will not have my hate. (...) Of course I am devastated by the pain, I give you this small victory, but it will be short-lived. (...) We are two, my son and I, but we are stronger than all the armies in the world. I don't have more time to spend with you; I have to raise Melvil, who has awakened from his nap. He is just 17 months old; now he will eat his snack like every day, and then we will go to play like every day; and his whole life this child will face will be happy and free.

Recognizing your own vulnerability is critical so that fortitude arises as a possibility. First, the vulnerability involves recognizing that I am not God; in my condition I am a human creature capable of receiving a wound and making mistakes, often out of fear. In the New Testament, the book of Luke (22:54-22:62) gives us an illustrative example of this. Peter was considered a friend of Jesus Christ, and also his favorite disciple. However, the night that Jesus Christ is apprehended, Peter realizes his vulnerability:

[54] Then seizing him, they led him away and took him into the house of the high priest. Peter followed at a distance. [55] And when some there had kindled a fire in the middle of the courtyard and had sat down together, Peter sat down with them. [56] A servant girl saw him seated there in the firelight. She looked closely at him and said, "This man was with him."[57] But he denied it. "Woman, I don't know him," he said.[58] A little later someone else saw him and said, "You also are one of them." "Man, I am not!" Peter replied.[59] About an hour later another asserted, "Certainly this fellow was with him, for he is a Galilean."[60] Peter replied, "Man, I don't know what you're talking about!" Just as he was speaking, the rooster crowed. [61] The Lord turned and looked straight at Peter. Then Peter remembered the word the Lord had spoken to him: "Before the rooster crows today, you will disown me three times." [62] And he went outside and wept bitterly.

In a negotiation, to be strong, brave and courageous means to recognize that we have failed and heal wounds, i.e., develop in a positive way what you have previously tried to justify. This attitude determines the success of a long-term process. That negotiator will not only be

stronger, but will risk more in action, i.e., will be involved in the game more as a person.

The failed negotiations are the best experiences to learn what not to do and what to improve. Many years ago, in my first experience as a business consultant, a customer in Mexico did not pay as agreed. I told him that kind of treatment was not fair because we had made an agreement in good faith. His answer was blunt: "Justice is divine." Then I remembered the scripture from the book of Matthew: "Truly I tell you, whatever you bind on earth will be bound in heaven, and whatever you loose on earth will be loosed in heaven", and then I told the customer, "Therefore, you should worry more about not being right on Earth, because if you believe in divine justice, you have to put your hand in your earthly treatment." Finally, the person paid me with a bartering of something I needed, and that meant more and had more value to me than the true value of the services I had provided for him; however, the bartering was not as important as the services provided to my client. This was the first lesson learned—that you have to write an agreement to avoid conflict after finishing work; the second lesson was that we must always be willing to be flexible and find a solution to future conflicts.

Another example of an error in negotiation is when we expect a lot from the other side and we are disappointed by their attitude or behavior.

It is important to recognize that disappointment is relative to our own culture and expectations. If we analyze it from the culture of the other negotiator, maybe something that disappoints us is not as critical as we think. This flexibility of thought can help the negotiator not to fall into disappointment even though in their culture it is. A typical example is when a foreign visitor comes to our Latin countries; the most typical behavior is that we receive the visitor at the airport and manifest a culture of very special hospitality. However, when invited to a country in northern Europe, to give an example without stereotyping, certainly the Latin cultural expectation is being met at the airport as a courtesy. But in the culture of northern Europe, with a much more practical mindset, instead of going to pick you up they suggest that you take the subway or bus and will indicate the appropriate time according to the agenda. We must not disappoint ourselves, because every culture has its moments, situations and different ways of being hospitable.

The provision is reflected in the risk of action. The martyrs of Christianity have given great examples of fortitude, not so much for having resisted the onslaughts of their torturers as the fullness and maturity to have reached the willingness to perform an action which is the highest of any human being: to give life for another.

That wound allows the martyr to gain a more fundamental and deep integrity. It is integrity and not obtaining a short-term goal which makes humans act on occasion to enrich themselves spiritually and gain added value in their whole life.

In any negotiation there are intangible elements and

values that are cementing it, although not obvious to those who wish to take advantage of the situation; there are attitudes and virtues that cannot be improvised. The fortitude of a person is not defined by the difficulty of the project nor the effort you put into it, but by the firm attitude of making a transcendent good and ensuring the entire process is well-geared toward that goal. The fort-to-be has to appeal to discernment to perceive good, has to be oriented from prudence to get it and has to exercise justice to run it. Only in this way one can be really brave. Being strong means, therefore, being able to assess things fairly; otherwise, strength without justice becomes the lever of evil.

Caution and fear in more existential terms are not opposed to fortitude, since they are the result of our vulnerable condition. Being strong does not mean not to feel fear: a courageous person in the course of a negotiation is one that does not let the fear of not achieving the goal—getting a package of stocks at a certain price, for example, will force him to leave the good relationship he had with his counterpart, who is surely able to sell him the shares at a good price in the future. The most genuine act of fortitude is not so much attacking, but resisting. Therefore, patience is essential. A patient man is not the one who runs away to avoid confronting evil, but is the one that does not allow being conditioned or guided by this evil into a permanent state of confrontation.

Some union bodies actively lobbying the public and private sector crash down wrongly to exercise some kind of force, which like a boomerang turns against them, creating more problems rather than solving them.

Take the case of the longest airplane pilots' strike from the 90's: it lasted two weeks and cost hundreds of millions of euros to Air France. In addition, Air France was about to ruin their relationship with their partner KLM, as this airline threatened to break up the partnership if the three thousand pilots of Air France did not stop the strike. The pilots of Air France, with all their benefits and privileged wages, worsened the situation and put at risk their jobs and those of the employees of the company, because after that year the airline reported heavy losses. The aim of the strike was to exert pressure to force the Franco-Dutch partnership to revise their expansion plans of the new company low-cost, Transavia, because there was fear that it would cause low wages and worsen working conditions for them. KLM's intention was to reduce costs and improve efficiency and results, but after the strike, negotiations for the next few years may have regressed and caused the mass dismissal of employees. The main criticism was toward the French pilots for not having agreed to work longer hours, as did their counterparts, the Dutch union, who had accepted the conditions. Patience is transformed into fortitude if one can keep the judgment, discernment and clairvoyance, even when one is the subject of a business "mistreatment."

A very different case is that of workers in a company in Japan, which despite entering into an active strike conducted themselves with all professionalism and excellence. The problem was that the company was not complying with the payment of wages to their employees. The behavior of the workers eventually generated a greater psychological effect than if every day they had organized strikes during working hours. Well, patient is the one that does not allow anyone to condition or position himself. Giving a little more, going beyond "what must be done" will result in much more impact on the other. Truly, there is greater joy in giving than in receiving, but the *quid pro quo* is enhanced in some cases, as in boxers, which gives them more joy to give than to receive.

Transforming vulnerability into fortitude also speaks of how committed we are to our personal growth. I remember a niece from Mexico, who works in a travel agency, called my wife Marcela for help. One of her customers needed a reliable driver to take him to Austin, Texas the weekend of Formula 1. The Mexican businessman who visited Texas in his private plane was having a difficult time finding someone trustworthy to transport him from Houston to Austin on those days. There were hardly any drivers available, as they were very well paid. One of my sons offered to work as a driver that weekend to generate income and experience something different. In principle, my son should receive them at the airport in Houston, then bring them to Austin at a reasonable schedule, to Formula 1. My niece told her client that her cousin was willing to serve as a driver. Her client, very happy, told my niece not to worry, that he was going to invite him to come to the events.

There is greater joy in giving than in receiving. Boxers Fresco. Athens National Archaeological Museum

The disappointment started with a change of plans. They asked my son first to pick up someone in San Antonio and then to take him to Austin. Then it was no longer the original plan to pick them up in Houston airport but rather at the Austin Airport. My son did not complain at all. First they told him that he would be taking a couple and ended up being nine people instead. Also, they wanted my son to take them around to parties and other events in addition to the Formula 1, until late midnight hours; a job that was supposed to be eight hours a day maximum became a labor of 24 hours in which not even a glass of water was offered to him. Before he left for the night, they asked him to be back at 9:00 am sharp at the hotel. But the next morning, before 8:00 in the morning, they called to say, "I want you here right now." My son was staying about 40 minutes away from their hotel. He hurried up to pick them up and when he arrived, they asked him to take them to a restaurant one block from the hotel, and my son had to wait outside in the car.

The end of his job was to take them to the airport in Austin, and once completed this, my son would return to Houston the next day to leave the car there. However, at the Austin airport they asked him to take someone else to San Antonio. As this activity was not scheduled, my son refused because he had a previous commitment.

To his surprise they left him without a car at the airport in Austin and said, "You're very a bad driver and here is your salary."

The truth, I was very happy that my son had an experience like this. It is hard, but it made him see that in life everything is not rosy and allowed him to experience fortitude. However, I wonder if for the Mexican businessman, once you have the title of chauffeur he assumes that the person can be mistreated regardless of his dignity. And I know Mexican businessmen who treat drivers as family and are friendly to them. For my son and for the whole family, this experience was very enriching.

We thank these business people that their behavior has given us the fortitude to overcome this type of action day to day.

AGAINST ANGER AND FEAR

I worked on an engineering and construction project proposal a long time ago with a client who had assigned to our company the scope of re-engineering services. The total investment of the services exceeded $40 million. After evaluating the project with an expert of our company, we would have to explain to the customer that to do a simple re-engineering project would not have significant impact; it would be unethical of us do the work without clarifying this issue with him.

The path to excellence in negotiation can lead us to transcend. The eagle is a symbol of excellence.
Illustration: Antoine Chamoun-Farah

We were about to reject a project of many millions of dollars for the company where I worked, but I had the fortitude to explain the issue to the person to whom I reported internally in the company. I was afraid of being fired, but I knew my responsibility was not negotiable. Fortunately, both my client and the people who I worked within my company had a very clear sense of ethics and professional values. If that were not the case, they would probably have accepted the job, they would have fired me or I would have resigned. As a result of our honest actions, a few months later we carried out a project of more than $100 million of engineering and construction services for that customer.

Being strong, tempered and ethical is very profitable in the long term. Fortitude must always aspire to be the shining emblem of the final invulnerability. As St. Thomas says, "By patience man remains in possession of his soul." And it's not about projecting an image of weakness. On the contrary, we believe firmly that this is to be really strong. The true strength, continues St. Thomas, is positively related to anger, for this works to attack evil and defend good. The courageous use of anger has no other value than a "temporary emergency resource," for example, the memorable moment when Jesus entered the temple of Jerusalem and used anger to evict the traders who had made this sacred place in a profane place. Anger, therefore, is an educational resource and not a relief or violent exercise of power.

Many negotiation tactics, like getting up from the table,

are not necessarily heavenly music. In some countries they use harsh tactics such as intimidation, pressure of time, lack of resources or availability. I have seen cases where before entering to negotiate, the other yells, puts a gun on the table or even strikes the negotiating table hard with his hands. What to do in this case? In my experience and depending on the culture, you can use humor, ask questions or remain silent to handle the conflict. According to Thomas Kilmann, depending on the relative importance between the relationship and the result, avoid, collaborate, compromise, delegate or compete are the types of conflict management strategies we use. For example, if the result and the relationship is not as important, then it is appropriate to avoid; if the relationship is more important than the result, it is advisable to delegate; if the result is more important than the relationship, you can compete; and if the relationship and the results are equally important, it is best to collaborate. In the middle of the following graphic, the style would be compromising.

In any dealings between two parties different interests are mixed in terms of passion, courage to face insults or facing your gut feeling. The inability to deal with these differences leads to neurosis and pathology, almost always associated with egocentrism. The need to impose or control the other is a defense mechanism. According to psychiatrist Franz Kunkel, "the the more serious risk one is exposed to, the greater the concern with which protection is sought." When feeling at risk, there is a disturbance in the psyche that can cause distress.

```
                    > Important
                    Relationship

         Delegate        Collaborate

                    Compromise
                                    Results
    < Important                         > Important
            Avoid       Compete


                    < Important
```

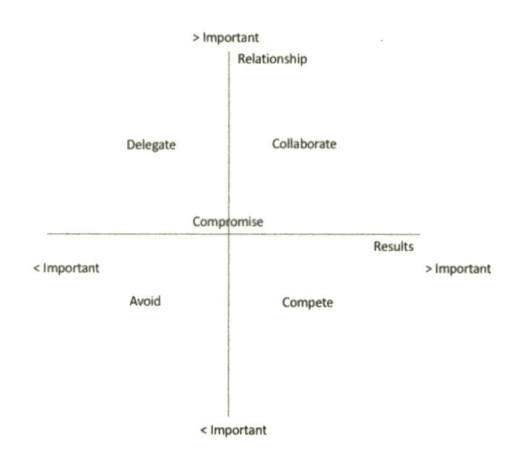

Relationship vs. results: conflict management styles according to Thomas Kilmann.

It is vital to have the courage to face any enterprise, regardless of the risk. A misplaced person who conducts egocentrically, seeking safety at any price and absorbing completely all his faculties, sooner or later will fail. The story of Schindler, the Austrian entrepreneur who helped Jews during the Second World War, shows us that how to save a single Jew the horror of the ignominious death became an infinitely higher good than to continue growing his business wealth thanks to the free labor of Jewish workers provided by the nefarious Nazi regime. We are convinced that the kind of strength practiced by the Austrian entrepreneur is the most appropriate tactic to transcend the negotiation. This fortress is the budget of a powerful creativity and wisdom that goes beyond any stereotype.

From an anthropological conception, every human being has an instinct for justice and truth, a first perception that can be considered as *semina verbi*. The term is the Latin translation of the Greek word *logos spermatikos* or seed of logos, present in human reason. St. Justin the philosopher said, back in the second century, that the *logos spermatikos* is the human impulse to investigate and become interested in knowing the truth, and this condition is available to us to meet transcendence. The father of anthroposophy, Rudolf Steiner, offered at a conference in 1908 a great example to understand why human beings seek virtue:

I have here a flower before me. This corolla, these petals, what were they a short time ago? A little seed. And in the seed, this white flower existed in potentiality. Were it not there potentially, this flower could not have come into existence. And whence comes the seed? It springs again from just such a flower. The blossom precedes the seed or fruit and again in like manner the seed, from which this blossom has sprung has been evolved out of a similar plant.

Thus these followers of the Logos-doctrine observed the human being and said: If we go back in evolution, we find him in earlier conditions still mute, still incapable of speech. But just as the seed came from the blossom, so likewise the mute human seed in the beginning had its origin in a God endowed with the power of uttering the "Word." The lily-of-the-valley produces the seed and the seed again the lily-of-the-valley; in like manner the divine creative Word created the mute human seed — and when this primeval creative Word had glided into the human seed, in order to spring up again within it, it sounded forth in words. When we go back in human evolution we meet an imperfect human being and the significance of evolution is, that finally the Logos or Word which discloses the depths of the human soul may appear as its flower. In the

> *beginning this mute human being appears as seed of the Logos-endowed human being, but, on the other hand, has sprung from the Logos-endowed God. The human being has sprung from a mute human creature, not gifted with speech, but: In the beginning was the Logos, the Word.*

If virtue is the acquisition of a good, fortitude is not the result of going through difficulties or effort, but to acquire a good. Mother Teresa of Calcutta, for example, looked for the good of people and negotiated worldwide fighting against poverty; capturing a good is what made her strong, and not the practice of negotiating with presidents and leaders. The strong perceives a good without inferring, oriented from prudence and executed with virtues. Without justice, the force gives distrust and lack of credibility, the opposite of the *Tradeables*. Force without justice becomes an anti-*Tradeables*, a lever for evil.

Caution and fear are not opposed to the fortress. In fact, having guts is going against fear, but not with the style of some people or governments that, "to combat insecurity," have weapons at home and fill the streets with police. Experiences of social work in Brazilian favelas showed that while invested in fear and trying to fight crime with weapons, it did not decrease but made the community weaker, as they sowed distrust among them, criminals or not. An urban agriculture program called "Gardens of Peace" changed this situation.

Authorities began training women and elders of the favelas in how to sow the land and seize any available space (ridge, medians, obsolete planters and vacant land) to grow food together. This project attracted women, children and youth at risk, led them to meet to work together the earth, to have eye contact and support to produce healthy foods that will palliate the lack of place. Investing in community gardens was much more effective than investing in weapons and police fear.

To be bold, doing good need not be reduced to the tangible and material; the most genuine act of fortitude is not attacking, but resisting, and beyond, collaborating. Consider that the rules and ethics are like a river with very specific channels. The river has depth and strength because it is framed in by the banks; without them there would be flooding of the surface. The banks are the rules and laws; they have clear limits of responsibility and give us an ethical framework on which to move with depth and speed. Depth is the truth; speed is justice and solidarity. The more limited the space through which water flows, the more power and depth generated in its channel.

Regulations and ethics are a river with very specific channel. Gave River, Lourdes, France.

GRATITUDE, GRATUITOUSNESS AND FORTITUDE

> *Draw me after you: let us make haste. The king has brought me into his chambers. We will exult and rejoice in you; We will extol your love more than wine; rightly do they love you.*
> The Song of Songs 1:4

In his book *Leadership, Jesuit Style*, Lowney describes how the missionaries of this order came to many populations and from the culture of others worked to bring them to a point of greater progress. Among these missions, he highlights the introduction of Catholicism in China. The history of the Jesuit St. Francis Xavier is an example of the strength that leads someone to take risks at all times, until the last days of his life. Angel Peña, meanwhile, considers St. Francis Xavier the patron and founder of the Jesuit missions in Asia (along with St. Therese of the Child Jesus). Although foreigners were sentenced to death in China, St. Francis Xavier went to that country as a missionary. There he founded several schools for the instruction of abandoned children and young adults in the main fortresses of the Portuguese to educate them in the human and Christian knowledge. He emphasized the importance of learning of indigenous languages and translated the truths of faith into the Tamil, Malay and Malabar languages, in rhyme so the natives could memorize it in song.

With the help of Anjiro he translated the Christian doctrine into Japanese. His example of holy life won him respect with all, even with the Moors and pagans. Everyone called him the Holy Father or Great Father. He had no fear of death and risked his life in very dangerous missions, trusting in God's providence. He was certainly, as he is called, the giant in the history of the missions and the apostle of the Indies. In September 1552, the missionary came to Sancian, an island near Canton in which Portuguese traders were installed to make deals with the Chinese. Francis Xavier needed to return to the mainland, but no Portuguese dared to take him on his boat for fear of retaliation and imprisonment. Finally, the missionary died in exile in Cochin, China. Five hundred years after his death, in recognition of his work, his name remains very popular among the inhabitants.

What makes us strong in negotiating also is the gratuitousness behind our actions. By gratuitousness we understand the act of will that goes beyond the *Do ut des* (I give you, so you give me in return). Giving is an expression of self-realization, that is, the person that gives constructs him- or herself. In his book *Man in Search for Meaning*, the survivor of the concentration camps Victor Frankl says, "Only the man who transcends reaches his fullness." When we go beyond self-love, love and concern, we've reached a level of fulfillment and achievement that goes beyond the expectations of the human being. But gratuitousness implies fullness, because I can only give what I have and not what I need.

A rich axiological equity (valucs) facilitates the donation; hence the most generous cultures are those who have a more accomplished moral heritage.

Gratitude between siblings is a gift. "If we could understand it won't be necessary to forgive, Father Ignacio Larrañaga

On the other hand, gratuitousness rescues the positive outlook of the counterparty; it dignifies the person. By this we mean that the other is not the counterparty that I have to bend, but the opportunity for me to develop myself morally. Gratuitousness helps us mature because it is not getting short-term interest. Also, it provides a link through which the subject's volitional process is exempt from certain selfish skills. Under the business framework we must overcome teenage attitudes that lead us to deny the other party to highlight our own identity. The good negotiator operates differently, recognizes and affirms the other party to confirm himself, and gratuitousness is an effective means of achieving this. The maturity of the person is measured more by what he gives than what he petitions, because gratuitousness comes from an accomplished expectation, while a petition stems from a lack suffered.

Gratuitousness is supposed to perceive the value of something, but when it is incapable of doing so, we suspect that there is a lack of self-esteem. One needs more recognition in life than one deserves. By this I mean that when I am recognized under my professional achievements, I note immediately that that recognition does not make me feel completely satisfied; I need a recognition that goes beyond what my actions deserve. Hence the importance of gratitude, which completes the cycle of gratuitousness.

I am happy and I don't get angry when someone thanks me, even though I do not deserve it. To be grateful, one must also be sufficiently generous and have a positive view of oneself.

It is important to tell the other it is good that you exist, but it is also equally important to tell myself it's good that I exist. Because the other always exists for me. But to realize that the other exists, it is necessary to consider that I exist, not only for myself but also for the other, because I am a being in relationship and the relationship is constitutive of being. God is one, but is not alone, say the Christians. St. Augustine, in his comments to the Psalms, says, "There are many Christians who only give thanks to God when they progress in their business. They leave prison and praise God. Business goes well and praise God. Inherit property and praise God. But if they suffer some damage, they blaspheme God. What type of son are you that when the father corrects, you are bothered and saddened?"

The theme of gratitude also leads us to consider that one is always in "debt" to the other. For example, one is forever indebted to people who have transmitted to us the values of other generations. When I don't correspond to the other I am in debt for omitting it, and it will slowly internally erode my self. In a negotiation, if I owe something to the other and I have omitted, sooner or later it will turn against me. The parable of the prodigal son (Luke 15) illustrates this dynamic. One day a son wants to go to see the world and asks his father for his inheritance. The father gives it to him, and the son not only wastes all his fortune foolishly but forgets about his father's existence and remembers him only when he is hungry, as St. Augustine says. After a while, he decides to return to his father's house, more by necessity than by repentance or gratitude. When you are not giving the other what it corresponds (i.e., love and gratitude of the son to the father), the son's selfishness becomes his own gallows. However, the generous father is always ready to receive the son.

Moreover, before he comes home, the father goes out to look at the horizon to see if he is coming. An act of generosity on the part of the father allows the prodigal son to reintegrate to his household. In the negotiation when one party acts from generosity, one is able to integrate the other party in a higher level of relationship and connection on the scale of Lopez Quintas, unlike living as a slave of an egocentric structure within the same negotiation, as happened to the prodigal son.

What determines our ability for gratuitousness is freedom. Animals, for example, are not capable of gratuitousness because they lack freedom; an animal can be fast in the race and fast in flight, but is not capable of true fortitude that emanates from gratuitousness. The real strength is not enough in itself, but depends on a transcendent element. The human being is never self-sufficient; gratuity reveals its inadequacy and radical dependence. If I thank you, it is because you have given me something that I have not been able to give to myself. Gratuitousness also requires trust and trust comes from fortitude. When a person trusts, he is strong, because trust carries with it the hope that puts the human being in himself to know that there is something that always transcends himself.

Behind every test, there is always a promise of fullness that allows us to face the difficulty of negotiating with hope.

There is always a greater good behind what we experience as failure. Human beings never lose hope if they know that there is something transcendent that rescues them from the meaninglessness of a failed negotiation. Hence the importance of the transcendental fundamentals of negotiation. The fortitude always requires a certain overcoming of human weakness and especially fear. Brave individuals are needed not only in conflicts, but also in those other areas where obtaining an immediate benefit annulling the counterparty is not expected.

What other fields are covered by fortitude? Following the doctrine of Saint Tomas, the virtue of fortitude is found in the human being:

1) That is willing to *aggredi pericula*, or willing to confront the danger. We can say that a good negotiator is one who is ready to face the challenge.
2) That is willing to *sustinere mala*, that is, to endure the adversities of a negotiation for a just cause, for truth and for justice. Casiano said in the book Colaciones (16:23), "One must persuade oneself that sometimes one is stronger who knows how to submit his will to the other than the one which still defends his own mind." It is always important to get into the other's shoes; do not forget that fortitude without justice is a lever for evil, and that fortitude without prudence is not a stronghold.

What we need to avoid is not that the other side is defaming us but being a liar. That's the real fortitude. If you do not have enough strength to hold on to what slips through the truth, you will also slip with the other side and will sink the negotiations. According to Spurgeon, "the door to the temple of wisdom is the knowledge of our own ignorance."

PSYCHIC STRENGTH[11]

The concept of psychic strength, whose empirical basis allows us to see the level of human maturity, also helps us to develop positively what has hurt us or gives us frustration. One of the bases of psychic strength is resilience, i.e., the capacity that every human being has to react to adversity, transforming it into a challenge, recovering the meaning of life and emerging stronger from the experience. Knowing what this capacity consists of and integrating our tools of life contribute to enhance our profile as a strong negotiator with common sense and maturity.

An example of the most representative characters of resilience in humans is Nelson Mandela, who spent twenty-seven years of his life in prison on Robben Island for opposing racism and apartheid in South Africa. Mandela lost three sons and one great-granddaughter, and after being released and elected president, he devoted all his efforts to reconcile his country through sport, around the same rainbow flag and an ideal without resentment.

[11] Data from the thesis of Enrique Martin: "Pneumatology and Ignatian spiritual discernment," Madrid 2001.

While in captivity, when Mandela got the worst moments of abuse, he recited the Invictus poem by William Ernest Henley:

> *Out of the night that covers me,*
> *Black as the Pit from pole to pole,*
> *I thank whatever gods may be*
> *For my unconquerable soul.*
>
> *In the fell clutch of circumstance*
> *I have not winced nor cried aloud.*
> *Under the bludgeonings of chance*
> *My head is bloody, but unbowed.*
>
> *Beyond this place of wrath and tears*
> *Looms but the Horror of the shade,*
> *And yet the menace of the years*
> *Finds, and shall find, me unafraid.*
>
> *It matters not how strait the gate,*
> *How charged with punishments the scroll.*
> *I am the master of my fate:*
> *I am the captain of my soul.*

The title of the poem, in turn, is also the title of the latest film by Clint Eastwood, who narrates the victory of the South African rugby team during the 1995 World Cup and shows how that victory served as a rallying point for blacks and whites around a hymn, an illusion, a future and a president, Mandela himself—an example of the importance of resilience.

Currently, positive psychology—the study of the conditions and processes that contribute to optimal flourishing of individuals, groups and institutions—is seeking to understand the processes underlying the positive qualities of human beings. This branch of psychology holds that resilience has three characteristics: commitment, control of events and challenge ahead on changes in life. According to these postulates, there are three basic vital traits to build happiness:

- A life of pleasure based on joy, manifested in good humor, optimism and hope.
- A committed life, and tasks involved in work, love, relationships with family or friends.
- A life of meaning in the self-knowledge and use of our talents gives us a sense of belonging and leads us to serve something greater than ourselves (transcendence).

HOW IS A PERSON RESILIENT?
American psychologist and educator Martin Seligman, within the framework of positive psychology, says that a resilient person has seven character traits or virtues: wisdom, knowledge, courage, humanity, justice, temperance and transcendence. In turn, these are manifested in twenty-four strengths, including be curious and interested in the world; explore and discover new things; love knowledge and learning; acquire and master new subjects; have a critically

thinking and open mind; have judgment and examine all the meanings and nuances; willingness to change their own ideas based on evidence; have creativity, originality, inventiveness and practical intelligence; devise new and productive ways of doing things; include artistic creation; ability to take perspectives; giving advice to others; find ways to understand the world and to help others understand.

Resilient people also possess or develop emotional strengths that facilitate the achievement of goals in situations of external or internal difficulties, for example:

- Boldness against threat, change, difficulty or pain.
- Ability to defend the position that one believes is right and act on own convictions even if it means criticism.
- Perseverance and diligence to persist in an activity even if there are obstacles, to finish what you start, and also to get satisfaction from undertaken and successfully completed tasks.
- Integrity, honesty and authenticity to always behave according to truth without being pretentious, taking responsibility for one's feelings and actions.
- Vitality and passion for things to face life with enthusiasm and energy, acting with conviction and dedication, living life as an exciting adventure.

The person with high resilience has three types of interpersonal strengths:
a) Humanity: befriend and love others, love, attachment, ability to love and be loved, to have valuable relationships with other people, particularly those in which affection and care are mutual.
b) Empathy: kindness, generosity, tendency to favor, help and care for others.
c) Emotional Intelligence, personal and social: be aware of the emotions and one's own feelings and those of others, knowing how to behave in different social situations with appropriate empathy.

Resilient people have a strong sense of civism and have strengths that are manifested in a life of healthy community, including justice, citizenship, civics, loyalty, ability to engage teamwork and group dynamics. The sense of justice and equity leads us to treat all people as equals; leadership makes us encourage and guide the group of which one is a member for common projects and strengthening relations.

A resistant person also has high rates of moderation, manifested in four strengths that protect against excess:
1. Ability to forgive and give a second chance without giving in to revenge and spite.
2. Modesty and humility to let others do the talking about oneself without seeking to be the center of attention or considered more special than others.
3. Prudence, discretion and caution in decisions not to take unnecessary risks.
4. Self-control and self-regulation of one's feelings and actions, maintaining discipline and control over impulses.

Finally, today we know that the resilient person has a high rate of transcendence, expressed in five strengths that forge connections with the immensity of the universe and provide meaning to life:
1. Appreciate the beauty of things, capacity for wonder, interest in nature, art and science.
2. Gratitude, manifested in the ability to thank a higher power for good and not so good, besides being grateful to others.
3. Hope and optimism to work with projection toward a better future.
4. Sense of humor, like to laugh, jokes, smiles and sees the positive side of life.
5. Spirituality, faith or religious sense.

These are some models and features of human maturity that could be multiplied. Human maturity consists of the coherence between what is and what is professed, and has its most convincing external expression in fidelity and responsibility in fulfilling the commitments and obligations undertaken with God and with other beings. You need to make a constant effort to make prudent decisions and definitive choices, and thus achieve stillness of mind to integrate with serenity emotional forces under the guidance of reason, will, faith and charity, openness and constant giving to others, without exception of persons, and righteousness in judging people and events of life.

Maturity is not a quality formed by several aspects. It is a range of attitudes towards life. The Second Vatican Council describes it as stability of spirit, ability to make wise and prudent decisions and a righteous mode of making judgments about events and men. These features are very useful for assessing the maturity of a good negotiator. It is about general and descriptive features that reflect, in any case, an existential maturity of life experienced.

It is possible that existential maturity may never reach a level of fullness in life, regardless of how old you are. This type of maturity involves taking a fundamental and essential responsibility for our own lives and about who we are, so that our passage through life is an evolution, a gradual development that brings to the world all the potentialities and capabilities sleeping within our deepest self that have not yet seen the light.

A comprehensive view encompasses structural maturity, that is, to know the role of the contents expressed in these traits within the global dynamics of each person.

As a cognitive subject, each person opens to the importance of knowing the meaning of things and the mystery of his existence. As an acting and free subject, the person is confronted with that freedom. And as an entity consisting of different levels of motivation, you are invited to integrate them hierarchically. In other words, the human being transcends acting from knowledge, freedom and necessity.

Fortitude is measured by the ability to build bridges in an area ruled by fragmentation, as in the case of business. A bridge is the opposite of an assault or a landing; it is not homogenization imposed, nor is it to reduce the counterparty to nothing. The negotiator who walks in humility is free from the need to resort to its position as a platform to take revenge on those who have taken advantage of him. Fortitude, justice, temperance and prudence, with humility, serve as a brake and equilibrium in a good negotiation.

REFLECTION EXERCISE

HOW MUCH FORTITUDE DO I EXERT WHILE NEGOTIATING?

1. Do I invest all my talents into a negotiation?
2. Am I able to tolerate suffering in the negotiation?
3. Am I able to value what is fair or unfair?
4. Am I patient when I know more than the other party?
5. Am I free from stereotypes of others in the negotiation?
6. Am I able to integrate losses in a positive way and make sense out of them?
7. Have I questioned myself on what is not negotiable?
8. Do differences exist between relative and absolute values in my life?
9. Do I have conviction in the negotiation?
10. Do I have many doubts and skepticism during negotiation?

% of Fortitude = number of YES / 10 * 100 = _____ %

CHAPTER V
TEMPERANCE

Temperance is the moderating virtue of wisdom.
Vatican Museum.
Photo: Habib Chamoun-Farah

> *There is a rebuke that is timely,*
> *and there is the person who is wise enough to keep silent.*
> *How much better it is to rebuke than to fume!*
> *And the one who admits his fault will be kept from failure.*
> *Some people keep silent and are thought to be wise,*
> *while others are detested for being talkative.*
> *Some people keep silent because they have nothing to say,*
> *while others keep silent because they know when to speak.*
> *The wise remain silent until the right moment,*
> *but a boasting fool misses the right moment.*
> *Whoever talks too much is detested,*
> *and whoever pretends to authority is hated.*
> **Sirach 20**

WHAT IS TEMPERANCE?

When we see that someone is able to harmonize what at first glance is disparate and divergent, we say something like, "This person has been able to temper a situation." Complex situations, in addition to requiring temperance, lead us to set limits and slow or stop certain voluntary actions. When we incorporate temperance in such a *sui generis* (unique from Latin) area as negotiation, a field where tension and conflict always prevail, we must recover the deep and anthropological sense of this virtue, which has fallen somewhat into disuse; however, this doesn't mean that it is not necessary or even providential.

Temperance is the virtue of moderating human wisdom. When someone is tempered or is exercising temperance, or has temper, as they say more colloquially, the first verifiable effect is his *animi quies*, i.e., the stillness of spirit of which scholars spoke, understanding the spirit as the soul. Temperance is therefore a matter of operating or realizing order in the personal sphere itself—"the cosmos," as the Greek philosophers said.

Temperance is the act of creating order in our own self, a kind of self-preservation, a habit that defends and protects us from ourselves, due to the fact that humans have a strong tendency of going against one's own nature.

In a practical sense, to be tempered is to have willpower, self-control, and the ability to set limits. It is not being cold, indifferent, or mediocre, but it is how to get the right balance in a negotiation and to identify if the process is carried out correctly. A temperate person will prefer, for example, to invest in a conservative product and to give up getting greater benefits if this translates into being faithful to his customers. A lack of temperance would be equivalent to depersonalizing a business in order to receive huge sums of money. "We cannot be like those men who appear to be guided by the economy, so that almost all of their personal and social life is dyed with a materialistic spirit."[12] When we put economic goods as the end goal and think that in them we can find happiness and fulfillment, we are filled with anxiety about acquiring them, easily forgetting the meaning of negotiation, which is the integral enrichment of mankind.

---

[12] COSN VAT 2, Constitucion Gaudium et Spes 63

When we talk about temperance, we assume that the goods which we use in the negotiation are objectively good, and to that extent are to be handled. When the means are not used as instruments, they become tyrants and enslave. Therefore, for a good negotiation, we must practice exercising temperance. The habit gives instrumental value to the means and avoids excess (characteristic of the consumer society). It helps us to do without the superfluous and to moderate ambition. Temperance returns to man the dominion over things.

You cannot be a really prudent nor an entirely fair and strong negotiator without the virtue of temperance. This indirectly affects all other virtues, but all other virtues are indispensable, so that the human being can be moderate in the use of the medium. The Moderate is the owner of himself; here passion does not achieve superiority over reason, will, and heart. That is, the fundamental and radical value of the virtue of temperance is indispensable for humans to achieve fullness. Just look at people who have started a business and have been washed away by their passions, becoming victims and renouncing the use of reason. Passion ruling over reason, however, has nothing to do with that healthy dose of passion that every entrepreneur needs to develop a business.

A manifestation of temperance in the business world is the ability to save, because it requires an exercise of planning and organization involving reason and will. Those who plan have a vision, and not a short-term horizon, and choose this avenue by virtue of the goals that savings project. The savings mindset with a long-term vision casts a positive outlook concerning reality, recognizing that the instrumental value of money goes beyond its accumulation. That is, the ultimate goal is not the ambition to accumulate out of greed, but rather, to obtain a greater good. Collateral savings creates opportunities for participation and a network of solidarity that works regardless of your current economic level. For example, a Spanish company for social economic investment and cooperation helps people in the lower socio-economic levels to develop the habit of saving. This is capable of generating synergies within a homogeneous environment of people who have common fundamental purposes, although different needs or interests.

By exploring temperance, we enter the emotional dimension of the human being—one of the most complex and least understood in the business world. It is vital that this human dimension is well-ordered and assembled. Although we are all susceptible to disorder, according to St. Ignatius of Loyola, there are spiritual exercises that allow us to order the affections.

Temperance acts in the psycho-affective or volitional structure of man as a kind of hinge between what is understood and what is done. In other words, I can have a clear understanding of all preparation tools that come into play during a negotiation. I can have an experience that allows me to get ahead in a deal, being economically successful in my predictions. I can have excellent training and a higher intellectual level, which, in principle, gives me advantages in the pursuit of the ultimate objective of getting the deal. However, that gift of intelligence requires me to have a well-forged will, that is, volitional mechanisms to implement these performance criteria. Without enough affection or tranquility of mind, harmonious activity would not be feasible to activate my potential to go beyond the inherent conflict in the negotiation. The opposite of this stillness of mind can be a gridlock or trap in dealing with others, because if not moderated effectively, I can disrupt the harmony of the other and from the subconscious create a barrier in the negotiations.

The National Organization of Blind Spaniards (NOBS) organizes an annual raffle, and blind people are responsible for selling tickets. Maybe you are not the lucky one that gets the prize, but the relationship with the blind person is more valuable than any final prize, because by doing an exchange with that person, we are reminded that the sense of touch and physical contact, which we often take for granted and to which we attach little importance, have enormous emotional value in human relations. This becomes more evident when we work with people from other cultures. For example, in the Arab culture, physical space between two people is so close that it can feel invasive and intimidating. Something similar happens with certain Latin cultures, where hugs are part of the camaraderie and confidence building, something very different in relationship building with people from "colder" cultures in which physical contact or closeness to talk is taken as a lack of respect.

In negotiation situations, we need to integrate the emotional and cultural dimension to avoid falling into misunderstandings. Temperance, or self-control, is a virtue that integrates all the faculties of the human being in a harmonious way. Sensitivity is one of those faculties. Touching, persuading with your hands, takes you to the subconscious and coordinates verbal with non-verbal. This interaction brings into play the discernment that allows us to separate healthy and unhealthy elements, knowing what is good for both and what is not. This is absolutely necessary to make a fair and informed decision that is not dependent on the actors or to make a preliminary discernment to understand from where and how to perceive those involved. The lack of discernment obscures the will, reason, and ethics, because to discern is to discover the truth, to understand what is most convenient, and to execute righteousness.

TWO ETERNAL LOVES

I want to share a story where I was able to integrate my professionalism with my affections thanks to temperance and discernment. Although it is a love story, it is not just any story.

THE ACT OF FALLING IN LOVE

From an early age, my parents instilled in me the habit of traveling to all the places that our budget allowed. When I was a young teenager, thanks to my parents, I had the good fortune to meet my two loves, two cities that I will never forget. The adolescent love I felt for these two places has not faded with the passage of time. On the contrary, it is similar to my feelings for my one true love, my wife Marcela, whom I met at an older age—the more I know her, the more I love her. The same happened with these two cities, two ports on two different continents. I fell in love with them without understanding why. Now, after almost 40 years, the love affair continues with a more intense passion.

The first place is called Cadiz, Spain. As a teenager, being on the seafront in a Phoenician port marked me for life, but I remember even with more excitement the first time I found a Phoenician sarcophagus of a male at the Museum of Cadiz, who, at that time, was the only one discovered in the port.

Anthropoid sarcophagi, Phoenician Museum of Cadiz, Spain.

First love, Caleta Beach, Cadiz, Spain.

I did not know if fate would bring me back there again. A similar situation would be an attraction to a person in a distant country without foreknowledge if you will ever see them again. While memories often fade, it was not the case with Cadiz, that magical place. The same thing happened to me with a Mexican port as a teenager. To me, this port had it all— Puerto Vallarta, Jalisco. Despite knowing other fabulous destinations in Mexico, there was something enchanting about that town that I will never forget.

Similarly to Cadiz, Puerto Vallarta had the sea, the harbor, and, above all, friendly and great people. I was very shocked by the kindness shown, aside from the great places to fish and downtown shopping. Puerto Vallarta has an inexplicable charm, and although I had not returned until recently, I have very pleasant memories positively etched in my life.

Second Love, Puerto Vallarta, Mexico.

THE PASSION

Some think that passion is momentary and ephemeral, but the kind of passion of which I am speaking is not delivered quickly. It is the kind of love that endures and excites you more as you discover more about the other. Instead of forgetting, you begin to create fantasies, and as long as your expectations are not deceived, passion increases. It's something I've only experienced with my family, with my work, and with these two cities. I wonder what fuels the actual fascination with these cities, but I can interpret my own experience. In life, what you love is what you find connected with your "Self". When you enrich your "Self", you are full of passion, which no treasure in the world can buy.

Although I am a native of neither Cadiz nor Puerto Vallarta, the passion I feel for these two cities is inexplicable. Without initially knowing it, it became an engine that has driven my actions. One day, I was invited to Puerto Vallarta to deliver lectures. Unwittingly, I became a friend of the Puerto Vallarta community and continued visiting them, giving courses and talks to hoteliers, merchants and the community in general. Don Luis and his team, the *Vallarta Opina* newspaper staff, were very important promoters to make this happen.

On the other hand, my passion for the Phoenician culture led me to be appointed founding president of the Phoenician International Research Center (PIRC), whose purpose is to spread the Phoenician culture and protect Phoenician relics. Salim Khalaf, director and creator of Phoenicia.org, the largest library on the Internet about Phoenician history, contacted me one day, and together with Dr. Nick Kahwaji, they asked me to contact the paleopathologist of Cadiz, Dr. Manolo Calero, because there was a major discovery of a Phoenician underground city in the port of Cadiz. We wanted to propose that Dr. Calero and I work together to spread the news worldwide. After I contacted Manolo, we became great friends, and because of him I developed a great relationship with the chief archaeologist of the city of Cádiz, José Gener, now also a great friend, as well as his research team. When I shared my dream of returning to Cadiz with Marcela and our four children, Habib, Emile, Antoine and Marcelle, my desire was welcomed with great enthusiasm by all.

Visiting Cadiz again and rediscovering every nook and every corner of this fabulous place with great memories from my teens was an incredible delight. I met more friends, and I was quickly adopted as a "gaditano" (local from Cadiz) returning home. Don Enrique García Agullo invited me to give a lecture from my book *Negotiate Like a Phoenician* in Cadiz, a place that had been founded by the Phoenicians. Just imagine the thrill for me! It was on that trip when it occurred to me to put together my two passions, promoting a sister city agreement between Cadiz and Puerto Vallarta, inviting the world to know their benefits and to embrace historical tourism.

FINDINGS
This was a very emotional visit to the places that had

marked me from the perspective of a teenager, and now making a return visit with my teenage kids gave me a vision of doing the right thing. Manolo and José had invited me, along with my family, to explore the most recent discoveries of the city. What a beautiful surprise! I was in front of the most exciting thing that had happened to me since my teens. For the first time in my life, I was facing a Phoenician skeleton and a whole Phoenician city being unearthed from beneath the building of the "Teatro Cómico." We were fortunate to be among the first to know about this incredible discovery.

Teatro Cómico, a before and after. Source: The Journal of Cadiz, Virginia Leon. Photo Courtesy City of Cadiz Spain. Photographer Manuel Fernandez

The Phoenician skeleton, originally named Valentine (due to its discovery on February 14, St. Valentine's Day), was 2,600 years old. After undergoing several DNA studies by pioneers in the field, his origin and cause of death were unraveled. About 30 years old and 1.77 meters tall, Valentine was the son of a mixed relationship (a European mother and Phoenician father). This confirmed the Iberian integration of women in the Phoenician colonies to ensure reproductive viability of the group. Valentine had died violently during a fire, possibly during one of the sieges of the city of Cadiz, then called Gadir. Next to Valentine, remains of two more bodies were found, one of Phoenician origin and another that showed signs of a violent death. Valentine, who received the Phoenician name of Matthan, was then studied for his eating habits, many of them revealing more about his culture.

Further remains of the ancient city of Gadir were buried nine meters beneath the Puppet Theatre "Tia Norica". A complex system of excavation has revealed paved streets, houses, workshops, ovens, dinnerware, ceramics, a necropolis and even a fish salting factory dating from Roman times. This deposit, three thousand years old, unveiled the first period of commercial splendor of the present Cadiz. The new archaeological site has confirmed the founding dates of Cadiz and has ranked Gadir as an important center of trade in the maritime routes of antiquity, leading to the so-called Circle of the Strait.

"Citizens of Cadiz have always been aware of their Phoenician past and have made this past their own. When we have the opportunity to access this place and people understand and see what we knew according to legend, it will be really important." These words of Ana Niveau, Professor, Department of History, Geography and Philosophy of UCA (University of Cadiz), led me to reinforce my desire to forge a sister cities agreement between Cadiz and Puerto Vallarta.

In the Teatro Cómico, built over the former city of Gadir, we find the remains of the Phoenician Valentine. Photo: Manuel Fernandez, courtesy City of Cadiz, Spain.

Vestiges of the ancient Phoenician city of Gadir. Photo: Manuel Fernandez, courtesy City of Cadiz, Spain.

Is it worth the effort without a clear path forward? I also wondered whether it was worth continuing to promote the Phoenician culture without receiving economic rewards, considering the cost involved for each trip. But something that reverberated in my subconscious generated enough energy to keep the drive going. Without having any tangible project or a business initiative, it seemed unwarranted to get involved in an outside business, but that's when discernment helped me to see why it was worth it, and temperance helped me to integrate my affections as an engine for the project.

PUTTING IN ACTION

What should be done with all the information found by archaeologists and researchers in Cadiz? How can we best show the world those wonderful discoveries? Through a project, *Valentine, the Phoenician Traveler*, we devised a route from Cadiz to Puerto Vallarta to tell a story of the discovery of America by the Phoenicians. The idea was spread worldwide to publicize both tourist and historical destinations. For this purpose, there was a video created at IMADEC University in Austria to bring information to the great museums of the world and promote the findings. My sincere thanks go to tourism delegations of Cadiz and Puerto Vallarta, since they were very helpful in providing promotional videos of their respective cities.

With the videos, lectures, and interviews on television, radio, and print media in Puerto Vallarta and Cadiz, both port communities were motivated and involved in the project. After much prodding and insistence, the Mayor of Cadiz signed a cooperative agreement for promotion between Cadiz and Puerto Vallarta. To reach to this point, several presentations were made in Mexico about the tourist destinations using the Phoenician route. In addition, we designed a master's study abroad course in international and diplomatic negotiations from Houston, with students from several countries, including Saudi Arabia, traveling to Paris, Madrid and Cadiz.

Then, in an academic trip for the MBA program, we

made contact with other organizations and signed a cooperative agreement to develop educational projects, sponsorships, study tours, conferences and seminars, including negotiation simulations from the ICONS project at the University of Maryland, a summer course focused on negotiations in cultural diplomacy with MBA students with the NOVANCIA Business School, a conference on diplomacy at the Embassy of Mexico in France by the Minister Jose Felix Poblano, and an intensive course on negotiation and conflict resolution at the CEU San Pablo Business School in Madrid. The study tour ended with a closing ceremony in Cadiz, where I gave a lecture called "The Phoenician Gifts to Humanity."

Meanwhile, in Mexico, Phoenician Cadiz findings were published, and several conferences were held in Puerto Vallarta on how to promote this city to the world. Thanks to the newspaper *Vallarta Opina* and Don Luis Reyes Brambila, several free lectures were organized to raise awareness of the new strategies of tourism promotion abroad, for example, making a sister city agreement with the city of Cadiz.

DISCOURAGEMENT

I had focused my efforts on promotional activities, developing relationships and reconciling the interests of those involved to sign a cooperation agreement between the two ports and spread the culture of both cities. However, after three years, I had only managed to get the signature of the mayor of Cadiz. To motivate the mayor of Puerto Vallarta, several publications were written promoting the city among students from Saudi Arabia, the military of Cadiz, and even Queen Sofia of Spain. In addition, the issue was presented at an international business forum for bilateral negotiations between Spain and Mexico at the Tecnologico de Monterrey Queretaro campus by the panelist Miguel Angel Fernandez de Mazarambroz Bernabeu, Consul General of Spain in Mexico. Despite this effort, we are still awaiting the signature of the mayor of Puerto Vallarta.

Temperance in this process of obtaining a "Sister Cities Agreement" has shown me that one has to be respectful of temporal processes to generate synergies, avoid voluntarism, not press negotiations that might precipitate an abrupt end, and add factors rather than divide the parties. To achieve empathy among parties, the virtue of temperance is needed. By this virtue, I have been able to summon willpower, always starting from the points of agreement and not of disagreement. The subjective truth determines an objective view of reality, which is why temperance, prudence, and justice help to act according to an objective view of reality, and not in discrepancy with it.

COMMITMENT

Despite disappointment, hope does not die, and the project continues. A negotiator is not outdone by a downward trend that gives life. No project is linear; there are ups and downs, and you have to be patient. Prudence and patience are imperative for a successful negotiator.

Even now, artistic and cultural exchange projects are in place between the two ports. A welcomed exhibition on culture is being contemplated in Cadiz. We have also planned a traveling exhibition on the Phoenician culture that would pass through Houston, the port of Veracruz, and other Mexican ports, before arriving in Puerto Vallarta in the not-too-distant future.

CONCLUSION

The most successful people in life are those who find their passion and follow it. If you manage to convey that passion to thousands of people, you are even more successful. In the case of Cadiz and Puerto Vallarta, all the activities that have flourished around the project have become more important than the actual "Sister Cities Agreement." The idea of touring the Phoenician route has already been promoted by City Hall in Cadiz. The project has been very successful, because it has attracted tourists enthusiastic about the history of this gem of the Mediterranean. Puerto Vallarta, in turn, has enjoyed a prolonged boom as a tourist destination.

Projects such as the "Sister Cities Agreement of Cadiz and Puerto Vallarta" may require many years to bear fruit, especially when governments change. For projects to be independent of changes of government is an area of opportunity in which we work. Temperance as a moderating virtue is very important for the negotiator in projects of this size, in which it is necessary to foster voluntarism and objectively reach solutions that satisfy most of those involved.

CHAPTER VI

DISCERNMENT

Knowing how to choose the road is important in a negotiation. Illustration: Antoine Chamoun-Farah

CHOOSE BY WAY OF DISCERNMENT

Today we are exposed to aggressive advertising that can be disrespectful to many groups of people. In addition to explicit messages, subliminal messages bypass reason and mobilize the primal and instinctive parts of a human being, negating objectivity and the possibility of rationalization. Today we also face a relativism that tells us it is impossible to know the truth, where everything seems to have the same value, because "what is good for you may be bad for me." At this point in history, we must pose ethical questions and recover the principles that are immutable, regardless of historical circumstances.

Discernment is essential in the process of understanding our reality. In Greek, *krinein*, which means screening or separating, refers to the psychological and spiritual discipline that allows us to distinguish thoughts and feelings and evaluate actions. It is the practical application of the virtue of prudence. Discernment helps us to make distinction between things that, *a priori*, seem to have the same value, but in fact do not.

Josep Vives, in *Principles and Fundamentals of Christian Discernment*, says that the human being has "the need to search for good and distinguish it from evil, the need to discover even more good than evil, to distinguish between good and less good, among the most good and optimum, from signs that come to us given by the same reality from outside and that are not simply chosen from each of us." So discernment is essential and constitutive for the human being to orient and act freely and responsibly in relation to God, if he is a believer, and in relation with the environment and with others even if he is not a believer. To live acting responsibly is to live humanly and discerningly in one way or another.

All human beings have the capacity of discernment. In exercising discernment, we use three of our dimensions: intelligence, affectivity and will. The ability to discern frees the subject, for example, from more or less explicit influence of harmful people. Hence, our negotiation model places more emphasis on the rational and emotional dimensions of the subject, while the purely instinctive behavior is to compete to win. Our model of the human being is not moved by blind or capricious instinctual impulses, but by a sensitive intelligence. Discernment has an instrumental value, not the end, but the means through which we are prepared to navigate to a decision. Choosing involves discerning well, so it is instrumental to a good negotiator.

There are four types of personal decisions that influence a negotiation:

1) **Preference**. In negotiating, a possibility may be selected not because it is the only probable outcome, but because it is preferred more than an affordable best alternative to a negotiated agreement (BATNA). On the other hand, the mature decision within a negotiation is based on internal justifications derived from an appreciation of what is chosen: I commit to

something because I believe in it, and that decision is born of my free will. Therefore, in a negotiation, it is very important to know my preferences and my motive for those preferences. The more moral capital I possess, the stronger will be my motivations, the more consistent will be my preferences, and the more transcendent will be my negotiations.

I remember when I was confronted with a decision regarding a Post-Doctoral position which I had the option to accept in France or England. Despite acceptance by the best universities in England, my preference was to live in France for the advantage of learning a third language. Inner motivation made me think and not doubt my preference. However, that preference did not eliminate the best alternative to a negotiated agreement, i.e., the possibility of going to England.

2) **Reluctance.** An impasse in negotiations, i.e., when you choose not to decide, indicates an improper process, but at the end of the day, it is also a decision. When the will is committed to a negotiation, it is better to say we cannot go forward than to give false impressions or make the other lose time without achieving concrete results. If I intend to give a constructive meaning to my day, for example, I must relinquish the desires that prevent me from it: sleep, fantasy, passivity, inconvenience avoidance, and so on. It is better to tell the other, "I'm not going to the meeting because I do not clearly see the objectives, and I prefer that we clarify first," than to be

noncommittal by saying, "Perhaps we can meet, but only if I finish my project."

3) **The relationship with the past.** Each decision in the context of negotiation, even one that seems banal or insignificant, has a pathway and a story that says something about us. It is inevitably linked with precedent actions or life experience. That is, when I'm negotiating, I merge in dialogue all my tradition, my parents' and grandparents' teachings and belief systems, with the present reality. We do not start from a neutral point, but from a story that precedes us, hence the importance of transgenerational negotiation. Keep in mind that there is no "small" option that does not condition subsequent ones. In negotiating, small gestures are very important. An insult to a customer, however small the incident, even if the relationship continues, will be a small stumbling block on the way to the next negotiation.

Another way to understand the transgenerational sense is this: when I am about to make a life or death decision, I wonder what my father, grandfather, uncle, or someone else I highly respect would do, leaving a mark on myself. My position in the past is a reference for my present negotiations.

4) **Orientation toward the future.** Choosing a negotiation is like designing a frame: it is necessary to determine the limits and distinguish the inner space from that which is outside. This interior space will fill future decisions. The condition of

commitment is very important, because it incapacitates the person to reverse decisions; you must maintain a clear attitude toward the chosen alternative and give up the other. Such resignation will give motivational contentment and joy to the alternative chosen. At the root of the decision, there is no mathematical supporting evidence, but only a free act based on moral certainty. If there is any residue of intellectual insecurity, it can only be overcome by trying and taking risks. Keeping the commitment is key, and it speaks not only of the integrity of the negotiation, but also of the negotiator.

I remember one occasion when I was invited to give a talk about negotiating to a labor union. The appointment was midmorning in a city near Mexico City. Only a few days before that conference, I was invited to a dinner in honor of the arrival of the President of Lebanon to Mexico City. The dinner was in direct conflict with the conference. Despite the personal importance and magnitude of meeting the Lebanese president, I could not attend, because I had already made a commitment to the workers' union. To my surprise, when I arrived at the conference site after several hours of driving, I found the union was on strike. Despite 200 confirmed conference attendees, the conference was boycotted. This made me very happy, because I fulfilled my commitment, and the responsibility was mine alone. What happened regarding the union was not a matter that I could control; they had an internal problem of commitment and loyalty.

A determined person usually has four characteristics:
1. Exhibits constancy and fidelity.
2. Is capable of withstanding adversity in negotiation.
3. Is an agent of social change due to both word and action.
4. Is relationally stable.

Embodied in a negotiator, these features translate into features of a systemic type that integrates the parts to attain the whole. In this integrative character, discernment is crucial:

a) **The good negotiator interacts well between the inner and outer world.** That is, he or she has the ability to deal with novelty and to automate tasks.
b) **The good negotiator integrates all intelligences.** We tend to associate this trait more with the IQ than the ability to learn and to adapt. Today, adaptation to the environment and the selection of the context are taking greater relevance, along with experience, in a negotiation involving several dimensions of intelligence (linguistic, logical-mathematical, spatial, musical, bodily, kinesthetic, intrapersonal and interpersonal, in addition to emotional intelligence). Therefore, to the extent that a negotiator can integrate these dimensions, he or she will be better able to discern and choose, because this diversity describes the complex human reality in a more perfect way.
c) **The good negotiator oscillates between two poles.** The good negotiator is reserved-open, submissive-dominant, sober-neglected, restrained-entrepreneur, trustworthy-suspicious, practical-imaginative.

d) **The good negotiator integrates the four cardinal virtues**: prudence, justice, fortitude and temperance. Thus, he or she better interacts with reality, integrating parts to the whole.
e) **The good negotiator is extroverted**. The extroverted negotiator is one who lives open, attentive and attracted by reality. There is a pedagogical principle that says "the opposite to being distracted is not to attract attention, but to be attracted." Negotiation is fueled more by attraction than voluntary attention, and in order to attract, you must connect.

An extroverted negotiator is able to establish connections with the whole, including primary traits of sociability, activity, vitality, assertiveness, dominance, sensation-seeking, and unconcern. Open-mindedness in negotiating implies, at the same time, a broad sense of aesthetics, i.e., order and beauty, according to St. Thomas, and the integration of feelings, actions, ideas, and values. Will or thoroughness of the negotiator is shown often in the form of competition, order, duty, need for achievement, self-discipline, deliberation and discernment. Extroversion incorporates in this process features of warmth, gregariousness, assertiveness and dominance of positive emotions. Sensitivity to interpersonal relationships is embodied in attitudes of trust, openness, altruism, conciliatory attitude, modesty and understanding toward others. The more neurotic the behavior of the negotiator (as opposed to emotional stability), the more this person will exhibit higher levels of anxiety, hostility, depression, impulsiveness and vulnerability.

Even with these characteristics, the negotiator loses his or her power if there is no order or procedure to achieve goals and bring stability to any negotiation process.

Here we contemplate at least seven steps:

1. Study a wide range of alternative actions thoroughly.
2. Be aware of the objectives to be achieved and the values that imply a decision.
3. Assess carefully what is known about the positive and negative consequences that may result from each alternative.
4. Find new relevant information to better evaluate each alternative.
5. Pay attention to any new information or suggestions from another expert, even when such information does not support the alternative that seems more attractive.
6. Before making the final decision, re-analyze the positive and negative consequences of all known alternatives, including those that initially were considered unacceptable.
7. Foresee in detail the implementation of the chosen action, paying particular attention to the necessary contingency plans in case any of the known risks materialize.

We believe that if these criteria cannot be satisfied, there will be failures in the negotiation process, and the more you work on these steps or procedures, the greater the chances of success.

DECISIVE STAGES IN NEGOTIATION

Discernment is the ability to prepare for the selection that can lead the negotiator to a better negotiation outcome. This series of stages, in our experience, will help the transcendental negotiator to better use the toolbox at his disposal.

Stage 1: Assess the New Situation
The process begins when a person is facing a challenge. He faces a new situation and asks himself honestly, "Do I take serious risks if I do not change my behavior?" If the answer is yes, the person begins to explore alternatives.

Stage 2: Examine the Alternatives
Once a person doubts his usual behavior will serve to meet the new challenge, he begins to look for alternatives that will lead to achieving the goals. At this stage, it is important to obtain valid information. For example, a couple of questions that should be asked are: Is this choice the best to reach the goal that I propose? Have I adequately examined all the options available?

Stage 3: Evaluate the Alternatives
At this stage, carefully consider the advantages and disadvantages of each of the alternatives according to the expected results and the likelihood of achieving the intended purpose. The virtuous and prudent person

makes an estimate of the pros and cons that may arise from the different alternatives and carefully assesses any new information, even if it does not support his initial preferences.

Some key questions suggested at this stage are: What seems to be the best option? Why? Does it harmonize with the trajectory of my life? What option is more convenient, not because I like it more or because it is more heroic, but because of its relation to all that I am as a person? Does the best alternative meet the essential requirements? If the best alternative is unsatisfactory, can I modify some terms in order to meet all the essential requirements?

This stage is where the typical symptoms of defensive evasion in its three forms frequently appear: defer the decision (decision making generates anxiety), delegate responsibility to another person (the insecure need to maximize certainty), or follow the easier alternative by justifying it by rationalizing (compensation of human needs not assumed, typical of the psychologically inconsistent person).

Stage 4: Reflect about the Commitment
Having made a decision, at least tacitly, go back to do it specifically. In this situation, the virtuous and prudent negotiator asks himself these questions: How can I implement the best alternative? What are the drawbacks or obstacles that can be foreseen? Should I inform others of my decisions? Sooner or later, the important people in your social environment will become aware. Their

possible disapproval could lead the negotiator to design certain social tactics and contingency plans to ensure the success of the decision. During this stage, the person who will make the decision also revisits the information gathered, contrasts it with the practical difficulties in implementing the decision, reflects about how to overcome them, and makes contingency plans should unforeseen setbacks arise.

Stage 5: Adjust to the Decision Despite Redirecting Feedback
The person usually feels happy after he has made a successful decision. This idyllic state sooner or later is tempered by setbacks, but the person ignores those who have little importance and tends to give a negative answer to key questions such as: Am I at risk if I do not change my behavior? If setbacks occur and the answer to the previous question is affirmative, this fifth stage becomes the first stage of a new decision; however, it is different from the original first stage, since the person has gone through the previous stages to reach a firm decision. When setbacks occur, you may stumble temporarily, but do not surrender and allow the decision to carry forward. It can be predicted that a person will remain indefinitely in the fifth stage until they find a difficulty large enough to cause an intense dissatisfaction with self or with the chosen behavior. Then they will restart the process in search of a better alternative. The stability of the decision will depend partly on the amount and intensity of reaffirming or redirecting feedback that the person encounters while executing the decision and his ability to tolerate it. The

more attention paid to the above staged activities, the greater your tolerance level will be.

It is not always easy to detect what stage the person is at, because partially resolved questions will leave doubts. It should be clarified that the stepwise process description developed can be misleading for two reasons: people do not usually work systematically and there is continuous feedback between the different stages. For example, a person can return from the third or fourth stage to the second.

THE NEED FOR DISCERNMENT

When you are faced with intercultural or interfaith situations, the need to discern is much higher. For example, if we have a meeting between Muslims, Jews, and Christians, how to integrate spirituality and know what to do and how to act with each person in a negotiation will depend on the level of religiosity, context, customs, habits and nationality.

From experience, I know negotiations differ with an Orthodox Jew, a Muslim or a Christian. Once, when I was teaching in Turkey, I heard my students stop to pray. This made me see a need to understand the spirituality of others and respect it, because it is something that you cannot negotiate. Something similar happened in the 2008 Olympiad in Jamaica. I was giving a course, but participants wanted to see the famous Jamaican runners who were in the finals to qualify. I was able to negotiate break time in exchange for another time slot. For some, sports is a religion, and for others, religion is a sport.

In the above cases, discernment is essential to avoid falling into a form of evangelism, which can be understood as a form of theological justification for how we perceive our own spiritual life and the expectations of others. In this process, we need to discern between the principles, the means, and the end, to understand limits, and to know what principles are not negotiable. As an extroverted negotiator would do, one must know how to move between the poles of innocence and naivety, which are similar, but not equal. In an intercultural negotiation, it is not good to start from suspicion, because it conditions the innocence and trust in the other. Although we show ourselves flexible to accept the right thing, in the negotiation, it is important to recognize that the right thing could vary for different people.

A transcendental negotiator seeks to integrate all the elements to act with justice and equity toward a common goal. In this process, it is better to be less perfect in unity than most perfect in division, as the transcendent elements in any negotiation are people and human values, not objects. The Phoenicians provide a good example of this transcendent vocation. They were organized into commercial enclaves that maintained relations with large cities in different ways. To expand their commercial activities, they formed alliances. Although they knew they were not always perfect, they recognized their value but preferred the relation above perfection. In appreciation of these trade unions, the Phoenicians built temples to their gods in every port where they settled. The great negotiators of Cadiz, for example, built a temple in gratitude to their god Melkart.

The great negotiators of history, the Phoenicians, had very clear vision of the relationship between spirituality and business. Do we, as the transcendental negotiators of the 21st century, have this relationship clear? Is a good negotiator necessarily someone spiritual? Is spirituality part of human existence? To answer these questions, we will briefly analyze several stories from different eras.

TWO WOLVES

An old Cherokee chief was chatting with his grandchildren about life.

"A big fight is going on inside of me," he told the children. "It is a fight between two wolves. One wolf is evil, fearful, angry, envious, painful, resentful, greedy, arrogant, guilty, inferior, lying, prideful, selfishness, competitive and superior. The other wolf is good, joyful, peaceful, loving, hopeful, serene, humble, gentle, generous, benevolent, friendly, sincere, simplicity, merciful, truthful, harmonious, compassionate and faithful. This same fight is going on within you and within all human beings on Earth," concluded the grandfather. The children meditated for a moment, and one of them asked his grandfather, "What wolf do you think will win the fight?" The old man simply replied, "The wolf that you feed will win."

This story tells us, first, of an inner struggle that we all share in common, because duality is part of our human nature, regardless of the culture in which we have grown up or the religion we practice. It is our power of discernment which helps us to distinguish which of the wolves we are feeding in our relationships and negotiations.

THREE THOUGHTS

The ancient historians say that there are three thoughts or motions that lead us to make decisions in the process of discernment. A motion is an internal movement expressed in purposes, inclinations, scruples, and so on. These three thoughts can be likened to three sentences:

- "There is one properly mine" defines my own freedom and love.

- Others are motions "suggested by the good spirit" that can be identified with God or meditations that make us grow as people and as spiritual Beings; these are the thoughts that manifest the will of God or the transcendent Being whom I ask for help.

- And others are motions "suggested by the evil spirit," those things that take me away from God and prevent me from doing His will.

In order to know whether we are properly distinguishing these motions in the negotiation process, we can ask ourselves the following questions: How much peace does this negotiation process instill in me? What, if anything, produces greater internal peace?

THE FREUDIAN TRIAD
The third story (philosophically speaking) brings us the division of the psychic apparatus proposed by the father of psychoanalysis, Sigmund Freud: Ego, Super Ego and Id.

- The I or Ego is the rational part of us that puts us in relation to reality and permits us to function in everyday life.
- The Super Ego represents all moral, ethical and social aspects of cultural thoughts received. It is the "should be." It consists of two subsystems: the "moral conscience" and the ideal Ego.
- The Id is the irrational and emotional part of our mind. It is the primitive, disorganized, and innate part of the personality whose sole purpose is to reduce the tension created by vital and irrational impulses, such as hunger, sexuality, aggression, fear, and so on. It includes everything that is inherited or that is present at birth. It is presented in pure form in our unconscious. It represents our impulses, needs, and most basic desires.

The I or Ego has a dual purpose. It realistically meets the wishes and demands of the Id and reconciles the demands of the Super Ego. As executor of the personality, the I (Ego) has to negotiate the demands of three forces: the world of reality, the Id, and the Super Ego. In addition, the I (Ego) has to retain its own autonomy and maintain its integrated organization.

The three thoughts from the time of ancient historians might relate to the division of the Freud's psychic apparatus as follows: the Super Ego would represent what the good spirit is suggesting to me; the ID would be the evil spirit; the Ego or "I" could be equated with the motions of the interior. This parallelism is not 100% precise, because there are vital motions of the Id that do not necessarily keep me away from God's will but are part of the system of human survival. Now, if we feed the ID excessively, then it will become the dominant wolf.

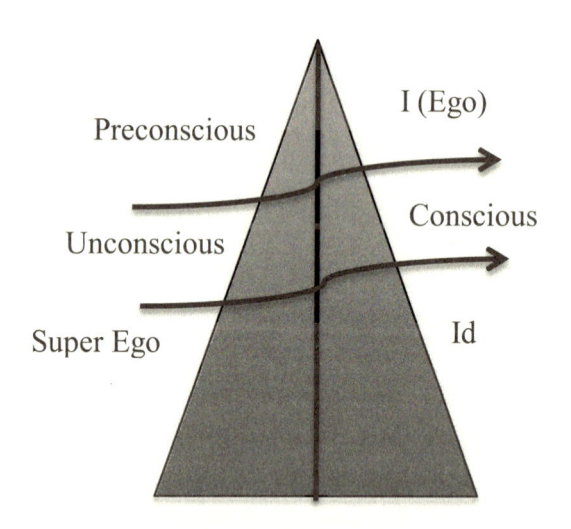

Preconscious

I (Ego)

Unconscious

Conscious

Super Ego

Id

The Freudian Triad

These three stories tell us about the spiritual dimension (anima or psyche) present in every human being. All three agree in one aspect: a constituent part of the spiritual dimension is the device or the ability of discernment. Regardless of the tradition from which we interpret spirituality, we must recognize that discernment is one of the ways in which this dimension is manifested, for without it, we would be unable to distinguish what brings us closer to or farther away from transcendence.

From various traditions of thought, we have developed a scheme that allows us to see how discernment works.

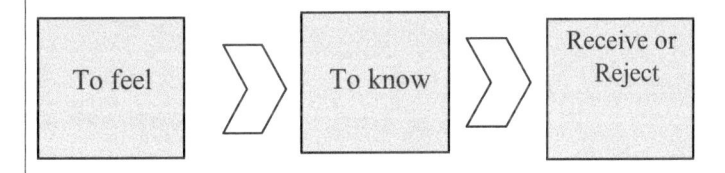

| To feel | ⟩⟩ | To know | ⟩⟩ | Receive or Reject |

Discernment Process

The first step is to feel (warning, detection, awareness, perceive the motions). The second step is to know and is the discernment itself (interpret, differentiate motions, understand, analyze and reconcile using analytical methods). The third step is to act (receive or reject, make a decision and implement it). In everyday life, these processes occur simultaneously, in an almost unthinking manner and within seconds. However, if we are to relate in a transcendent way, before acting we can ask the question of the ancient historians: How much peace will this negotiation process instill in me? To conclude this section, let me share one last story from the book *Un Adelanto del Cielo*.

It happened during a month of volunteering in the summer. When we arrived in Nairobi (Kenya), we wondered how we, inexperienced college girls, could help in dirty, dusty and hot Africa. Maybe we could fix roofs, but we had no experience in construction. Perhaps we could paint a school, but we did not know anything about painting. What we did have was a clear intention to give ourselves fully to others. However, we would receive much more than we give. We were lucky to get in touch with the Third World through a housing project for dying children of the Sisters of Charity in Nairobi.

We all entered that hovel, an unfurnished dump, in low light with spotless white and blue suits of the Sisters of Charity, brimming joyfully in contrast to the hammocks filled with sick, whimpering children.

I was frozen in the middle of the room. I had never seen anything like it. My university classmates scattered through the rooms, following several nuns who needed their assistance.

A sister asked me in English, "Have you come to look or do you want to help?"

Surprised by such a direct question and in a state of torpor, I stammered, "To help…"

"Do you see that boy there at the back crying?" He cried inconsolably, but without force.

"Yes," I said, pointing at him.

"Well, take him carefully and bring him. We christened him yesterday."

I noticed he was running a high fever. The child was a couple of years old.

"Now take him and give him all the love you can ..."
"I do not understand ... excuse me?"
"Give him all the love you are capable of in your own way."

And she left me with the child. I sang, kissed him and cooed. He stopped crying. I smiled. He fell asleep. After a while, I looked at the sister, crying. "Sister, he is not breathing."

The nun certified his death. "He has died in your arms ... and you've advanced him to heaven with fifteen minutes of your love, the same love that God will give him for all eternity."

Then I understood many things: the sky, the love of my parents, the love of Jesus, the details of affection from my friends ... My trip to Kenya marked a before and after in my life. Now I know we all have "Kenyas" around to give love every day. I will go through life once. Anything good I can do or any kindness I can do to any human, I must do it now, because I cannot pass back there again.

The story, told by Mother Teresa of Calcutta, tells us about a volunteer who went to help others, but ended up helping herself.

DAILY THERMOMETER OF NEGOTIATION

We should ask ourselves whether the negotiation or relationship in which we are engaging is going to help us transcend or if we are only acting to fulfill a transactional goal.

Among the tools provided to us, psychology is the proof of resonance and dissonance. In the context of this book, resonance is related to wondering whether the concepts presented here are echoed in me from a spiritual standpoint and not in the intellect. Resonance leads me to pay attention to feelings of the ancestral memory and heart sectors. In the experience of resonance, one feels reverberation within the body, spirit and mind. It may be something that we hear, something we read or something we see. Everything vibrates in unison, and it seems perfect. It feels like part of us, and we realize that this information we have available only appeared at that precise moment in time by the work and art of a law that goes beyond our understanding.

Energy resonance, according to the Larousse dictionary, is the vibrational response of a tuning fork when it is touched with a critical frequency. If we discard our intellect and attune our hearts, there are plenty of situations in which we can experience resonance. Certain things that resonate in me may not make someone else resonate and vice versa. The resonance test can be used in different situations in life.

Dissonance, according to the same dictionary, is the mismatch in the addition of two or more successive or simultaneous sounds. It is also the lack of conformity or proportion which some things must naturally have. Hence, sometimes we say intuitively, "Something is telling me this is not right."

I remember once I attended a congress for shopping center development in Las Vegas, Nevada, and all my colleagues after the conference decided to visit nightclubs. That group's decision was far from resonating in me. In fact, it produced dissonance in me, because it went against my beliefs.

The resonance test can help us discern an intuitive and emotional site that we often do not have access to consciously. When you're in a decision-making process, repeat this exercise throughout the process. Ask yourself the following questions:

- What resonates in me?
- What produces dissonance in me?
- What did not sound right to me?
- What is asking me to change my point of view?

Register your perceptions in this table, without judging.

	It Helps You			It Doesn't Help You		
Day	Predominant Feeling	Predominant Thoughts	Predominant Feeling	Predominant Thoughts	Observations
1					
2					
3					
4					
5					
6					
7					

Daily Discernment Table

Do not underestimate this information. Integrate it into decision-making process, and keep it as a thermometer of your feelings.

THE FOUNDATION OF INDIFFERENCE

I have lived in the United States of America for many years in a traditionally Anglo area. I am a member of a club where the ethnic majority is also white Anglo-Saxon. For several years, I have frequented the gym and sauna area. Every day for two years upon entering the sauna room, I have continually run into the same people, predominantly white men averaging 65 years of age. My custom always is to greet each with a "Good morning." In these 24 months, I continued to greet them each day although I never received a response.

One day my kids suggested that I no longer speak to or greet anyone, and so I didn't, though I had a hard time acting against my being. After three months, I decided I was not going to change my way of being kind because of the indifference of someone else. Upon entering the sauna and greeting one of the typically silent men, a strange thing happened. The man answered me with a throaty sound that sounded like a "mh." A few weeks later, another of the men actually replied, "Good morning, how it is going?"

I had always wondered why these people did not greet me. Did they not like me? Was it because I am Mexican? Are they racists? Were they mad people? Fortunately, I did not care whether they greeted me or not. My indifference (positive) allowed me to remain free to be myself and not act on inferences. Later on, someone told me that one of the guys that didn't reply to any greetings had a family member die a few years ago and had never overcome the situation. Therefore, when someone doesn't greet you, smile, or act according to your expectations, it's best to be indifferent and not take it personally. Unless you ask, it is difficult to understand what is happening.

In this context, indifference does not mean that I do not care about something. I feel neither disgust nor attraction, like nor dislike. Rather, my disposition is subject to conditions—something contrary to my inclinations. Indifference means that I act based on my inner freedom, following the will of a supreme being. I show availability at the time of an election.

Following the teachings of St. Ignatius of Loyola, indifference is a temporary resource that makes us start with a provisional neutrality before making a decision. The less conditioned the indifference is, the freer I will be. Among Mexicans, for example, there is a bias toward the inhabitants of Mexico City. "I cannot stand chilangos," say those who live in the provinces outside of Mexico City. This prejudice does not make you free, and you are not indifferent. Being indifferent would not be feeling repugnance at certain attitudes just for the sake of it, but for a transcendent purpose, to respect otherness and difference; I treat others as I would like to be treated. I refuse to act based on inferences that can ruin my everyday relationships and limit my possibilities. Being indifferent, in this context, means to be maximally free in the process of negotiation.

14 RULES TO NEGOTIATE WITH FAITH

This section is kind of a Vademecum, the guide used in pharmacies to describe the function of the active substances of medicines. To address the ethical dilemmas posed in a negotiation with a sense of transcendence, we have adapted a series of discernment rules developed by Saint Ignacio of Loyola, and we accompany each rule with a commentary.

Before getting into the essence of things, we start from a common base. The first step to become transcendent negotiators is to accept that our vital dynamic consists of various dimensions and motions, so we require a good deal of patience, flexibility and empathy in the learning process. The second step is to recognize that we live in a reality in which everything is connected and that the perception of these connections depends upon how open we are.

There are two types of people or spirits: those who go from bad to worse and those who improve every day. The messages gleaned in reading these rules will depend on each person's prevailing spiritual moment. In some rules we will provide examples for case A (those who go from bad to worse) or case B (those who are improving every day).

FIRST RULE

The tendency toward complacency of those who go from bad to worse can pervert success in negotiation. Being complacent makes us lose the ability to discern the dangers of misuse of the powers of negotiation.

In losing analytical capacity, I become a slave to my vice and lose bargaining power. The evil spirit paves the way of comfort and imagination to preserve and deepen the person in that state of vices and corruptions. His phrase is, "It's all good; everything is possible." The good spirit, however, pierces and gives a guilty conscience using reason. The good spirit says, "Something is wrong; not everything is good for you."

How do *spirit negotiators* act?

Comparison between Bad and Good Spirit Negotiator

BAD SPIRIT NEGOTIATOR	GOOD SPIRIT NEGOTIATOR
Inertia or tendency to appear superficial False expectations (deceitful promises) Increased vices and bad tactics Imagination without real support Re-start progressively toward failure	Develop Self-Criticism Reason Using awareness in Negotiation Someone who supports Self-Criticism or coaching

SECOND RULE
In people who walk caring for their spiritual life in negotiations and are progressing, the opposite of the first rule happens.

The evil spirit negotiator puts obstacles, remorse, consciousness, saddening and sowing, and unrest with false reasons to slow down the improvement. He says, "You see, you cannot do it; that's not for you."

The good negotiator spirit, however, encourages, gives strength, comfort, inspiration and stillness, putting aside what seems an impediment to the person so that he does not stop. He expresses, "You always learn something new and in a special way from failures."

Inferiority complexes in the negotiation are detrimental to the negotiator. It is essential to think about the negotiator talents to overcome frustrations and failures, as there is no time to get depressed. One must use the good or bad negotiator spirit marks left in the negotiation to determine the false reasons or mechanisms of self-defense and self-justification that hold us back.

A good spirit for a successful negotiation is well structured affectively, has emotional intelligence and iron will, generates bright ideas, has unity of heart, and is pure. When we negotiate in good faith, guided by the good spirit, we can more easily discern if the other party is going through a low or bad spiritual moment because of the sadness that shows, or vice versa. If we have good working relations, we must seek that the relationship is not perverted by the result and rather capitalize on the relationship to know the benefits of fair and just negotiation.

THIRD RULE
Before you start negotiating, you have to be sure of your mental or emotional tone.

The look I project toward others is a clean look that brings me to the service of the person. In the negotiation process I have to be clear about the purpose of the service I am offering to the other.

I remember during the World Youth Day, which took place in Madrid in 2013, more than three hundred thousand young people visited the city to listen to the Pope. There were groups formed of twenty people of various nationalities, for example, five Spaniards, plus other Frenchmen, Argentineans and Uruguayans. At night, around 10:30, the Spaniards proposed to the foreigners to go out to dinner. They came to a restaurant, but the gentleman managing the restaurant was in the process of picking up everything and closing for the night. When he saw that young people wanted to have dinner, he told them he could not serve them unless they helped him to pick up, because he was alone in the business. The boys willingly accepted. They had dinner, had a good time, and around 1:30 a.m. requested the bill. The owner of the restaurant told them that the dinner was already paid for. These young people, with their joy and service attitude, had restored his faith. The boys wanted to pay the bill, totaling about 300 euros, but the man said, "I lose 300 euros, but I won joy, positivity and conviction to serve with joy." Money was not proportional to the joy he had felt. Finally, it was like attending a group of friends.

Be careful, because euphoria is no spiritual comfort. The euphoria in the context of a negotiation is a feeling of complacency centered on self. Sometimes the thrill of success makes us dispense of other human dimensions like values or spirituality that make us consider others and respect ourselves. One must be careful with this temporary excitement and always seek an inner stillness.

Inner stillness is not experienced only on the surface, but throughout our being. Its features include intercommunication and durability, i.e., the fluidity and transparency of the deal that gives peace of mind to both parties. Stillness also has motivational force and is very powerful for the negotiation; it gives vital confirmation that I participated in an activity that joins the transcendent with the immanent, temporal and timeless. Finally, just as it is important to have a reference point when there is fog, stillness is a benchmark in the most difficult moments of the negotiation.

A foggy day in Quito, Ecuador.

FOURTH RULE

Learn to manage the failure of the negotiations.

In moments of failure we usually feel desolate. In a state of disorientation and confusion, there may be materialistic impulses, anxiety and temptations, distrust, despair, indifference, laziness, warmth, sadness, feeling the absence of a supreme being.

These feelings are very important; incubate these thoughts, and be wary of the thoughts that gain strength after a failure. Try to be self-critical in your reasoning during a negotiation, and remember that your mood is temporary.

The spiritual desolation is more marked by the lack of faith, hope and charity.

The temporal desolation, however, is characterized by a disintegration of the subject. The person feels coreless and without freedom. Sometimes, failure in the middle of a negotiation gives us a jolt that makes us aware that we need to restore faith in our abilities and future projection. Both sinking and this moment of frustration have in common the feeling of rupture and separation, like something is broken.

When it comes to a negotiation process, we must go back to weld what has been broken. It's time to introduce a good dose of gratitude in the relationship, invite the other for dinner or to the opera, and so on. At such times it is important not to make changes to the foundations of the deal; unreferenced in the fog, we run the risk of losing the way. Check what you usually do in similar situations, how you tend to react. Write down your reactions.

Negotiation is not a land without conflict; we pass through a process of internal and external struggle that can cause us pain. Sometimes we are more desolate in what we think, and we do not notice it. In my experience, the real obstacles of a negotiation process may be only the tip of an iceberg. When we begin to see them, we go from desolation to bewilderment.

FIFTH RULE
Learn to discern in bewilderment, but do not change in desolation.

In times of desolation you never have to make changes regarding the purpose or determination you had just before the failure. When you hear that voice that says, "Leave all, abandon all," stand firm and steady, because better times will come. As consolation guides and advises the good spirit, desolation is a bad counselor and worse friend.

Sharing a meal, dose of gratitude in the relationship.
Illustration: Marcela F. Chamoun

Following the success of negotiations, the positive feeling of consolation appears. Failure is a time of adjustment. Puzzled, we must not change course, because we can betray basic principles. The platinum rule is firmness and consistency. Resisting is to advance and to fight.

SIXTH RULE
Work without rushing, but without pause.

In times of desolation, we have to react internally and say yes to changes in patterns of thought and feeling that bring us the same desolation. Working slowly but surely allows us to shake off what deters us and covers everything with a cloak of sadness. Above all, reflect and examine more deeply to identify small things that make us "limp" and then "let's sharpen our skills." At this time patience should be increased in a convenient manner.

SEVENTH RULE
We always have the resources.

Those who are desolate know that it can be a test, within the limits of our natural resources, to resist the agitations and temptations of the enemy.

Remember that you always have the resources; the question is how to capitalize on them. How to capitalize on the resources of a good negotiation? What to do in a frustrating negotiation? First, one must know that one is always being tested and needs to value oneself. Second, look at the forest and not just at the fallen tree. In other words, do not dramatize, practice a helicopter view, take a sane distance from things, and things will take their proper perspective.

EIGHTH RULE
Work to exercise patience.

Those who are desolate have to work to maintain patience (as opposed to letting themselves be discouraged by the inconvenience that besieges them) and not forget that consolation will come, because there is no evil that lasts a hundred years. Negotiator evil spirit is impatient and is looking to make us impatient. But remember the words of St. Teresa: "Let nothing disturb you, nothing frighten you; everything passes; God never changes. The patient reaches everything. Who has God lacks nothing. God alone is sufficient." Being patient does not mean being resigned; patience is the domination of oneself, and it is active. Think of better times to exercise the hope that will come with consolation. Desolation closes the horizon, but patience opens it, and all this leads us to discover the cause of this failure.

NINTH RULE
In desolation, discover your responsibility.

What is my degree of responsibility for what happens to me? We are tepid, lazy or negligent when we do not want to accept the truth about ourselves or others. We do not accept ourselves, nor do we accept others as they are. Know your limitations, and do not react. Reactive choices make us gradually lose the sense of our mission. Negligence makes us blind to our weaknesses. On the other hand, lack of humility and sincerity are also forms of negligence. Let's not put our nest in a strange house, so that our concept of ourselves does not rise so much that it becomes pride or vanity. Failure tests us; it is a call to correct the intention and aim better in the right direction.

TENTH RULE
Learn consolation for desolation.

The one with a successful business has to consider what he did right in order to cope with future failures. The good spirit takes a moment to reflect upon the success of the negotiation. Before closing the case, ask the following questions:

What are my certainties and strengths at this time? What depends upon the immediate results of the negotiation? If this were my last negotiation, how would I do it?

Successful negotiation gives us learning and defends us against frustrations or failures that will eventually come. So in times of success:

• We must prepare, store light and strength, as Joseph did in Egypt when he was a slave falsely imprisoned before he rose to be the second in command.
• We should not believe that everything is solved; there will surely be some details to be fine-tuned in execution.

- Remember that there have been worse times. If we are sure of anything (simple probability), after consolation may come desolation.

ELEVENTH RULE
Try not to feed the ego.

Avoid thinking that we can do everything. Maybe if we have been victims of frustration, it is to put our strength in the resources that we still have. In the following table we see that with either success or failure, we always run the risk of feeding the ego. Success and failure are both feet that allow us to walk; they both complement and support each other and are the manifestation of a dialectical approach. Let's remember a good negotiation is not linear but has ups and downs. Neither increases nor decreases are important in the process; what matters is what you learn in the overall activity. Do not deny what we feel, but we cannot stay in that state of permanent desolation. The healthiest thing is to recognize what happens to us, write the lessons learned, and go beyond. If we react well, we will achieve giant steps.

Failure induces a profound change of attitude not to go through life with absolute self-sufficiency. We cannot attribute to ourselves all the resources nor worship our own self-perfection, because this leads to arrogance and selfishness and the ideal is never reached. There is nothing worse than believing that we are good and despising others; this is the breeding ground of dissatisfaction. Recall the case of the flight attendant: despite the insolence, it is best not to react or put yourself at the same competitive level as the other.

CONSOLATION – SUCCESS	DESOLATION – FAILURE
We must proceed with humility; prevent possible excesses, like making promises we cannot keep.	Do not get discouraged or collapse. (Assume errors with humility without dramatizing; everyone can be mistaken.)
One must be careful of pride when considering that success is only the fruit of our merit or activity.	When we need more value or courage, learn to ask for help (assuming that we cannot do it all alone) and lean on a supreme Being.
You have to live with the spiritual diary; remember the "lean cows."	

To understand the issue of dependency, we will explore game theory. This guides us in making decisions and shows that the decision of one depends on the decision of the other and vice versa. The typical **game theory** problem is the prisoner's dilemma.

The **Nash equilibrium** is, in game theory, a concept solution for games with two or more players. This assumes that each player knows and has adopted the best strategy and knows the strategies of others. Consequently, each individual player does not win anything by changing his strategy while others keep theirs. Thus, each player is running the best move he can, given the movements of the other players.

A **Nash equilibrium** is a situation in which all players have put in practice, and they know that they have, a strategy that maximizes their profits given the strategies of others. Accordingly, no individual player has incentive to change his strategy.

Meanwhile, the prisoner's dilemma shows that two people cannot cooperate, even if cooperation serves the interest of both. Albert W. Tucker formalized this theory based on prison rewards, hence the name of the theory (Poundstone, 1995).

The classic statement of **the prisoner's dilemma** is: Police arrest two suspects. There is insufficient evidence to convict them and, having separated the prisoners, visiting each separately, they offer the same deal to both: "If you confess and your accomplice does not confess, the accomplice will be sentenced to the full penalty of ten years and the first one will be released." If one is silent and the accomplice confesses, the first one will receive that penalty and the accomplice will be freed. If both confess, both will be sentenced to six years. If both deny it, all they can do is lock them up to six months for a minor charge.

Let us see this in a scheme:

	You Confess	**You Don't Confess**
Other Confesses	Both are sentenced to six years	You are sentenced to 10 years and the other is set free.
Other Doesn't Confess	The other is sentenced to 10 years and you are set free.	Both are sentenced to six months

Let's assume that both prisoners are completely selfish, and the only goal of each is to reduce his own time in prison. As prisoners, each has two options: cooperate with his accomplice and don't confess, or betray his accomplice and confess. The result of each choice depends on the choice of the accomplice. Unfortunately, one does not know what the other has chosen to do. Even if they could talk to each other, they could not be sure to trust each other.

The feeling of frustration in the negotiation is normal. In fact, if we do not experience this, it is a bad sign. What we must not do is be overcome by frustration. Sometimes the reasons for the frustration may come from external agents or those internal to us. Inwardly, it can be something in me that makes me feel stronger. For example, when you are in love, you face difficulties much better than when you are not. In conclusion, many times we are in this dilemma, and to solve it, we need to have the gift of discernment.

TWELFTH RULE
The enemy is weak against force and strong against weakness.

Three parables help us understand the deceitfulness of our understanding in a negotiation process.

HARPIES
Harpies strategy is to create fear and become discouraged with overwhelming force. Harpies appear in myths as huge winged geniuses (depicted as winged women with claws) to scare people and to seize their property. One of the best known stories is that of the harpies besieging the King Phineas, taking everything that belonged to him in front of him, especially food. What they could not carry away, they littered with their droppings. When the Argonauts came to the land of Phineas, the king asked to be released from the harpies. Zetes and Calais chased them to make them flee. These two Argonauts symbolize the strength and the courage required to confront the forces that grow uncontrollable problems, these pseudo-reasons that before the force of reason and of courage will weaken. Sometimes you have to do the exact opposite of what a prejudice or pseudo-reason is suggesting. It is the same strategy used with whimsical boys. They say, if you propose A to me, I'll do B.

THE DON JUAN
Don Juan is a literary figure originated by Tirso de Molina in his work *The Trickster of Seville* and recreated

by José Zorrilla in *Don Juan Tenorio*. However, the archetype of the Trickster already existed in the popular imagination before appearing in literature. His moralizing function, deeply Catholic, was to maintain life and customs within the established order, as Don Juan represents the breaking of the rules. For him, neither the church nor the moral of human justice had worth, because life was like a game that should be enjoyed in freedom—one of the oldest dreams of man, by the way.

To say that a man is a "Don Juan" is the highest compliment you can receive as a male seducer of women. According to experts of the Teatro La Paca (Jaen, Spain), the current reference to Don Juan is simplified and doesn't represent the complexity of the original figure, which portrays "the contradictory human condition: driven by selfishness, facing the essence of instinct with religious beliefs, behavioral norms and laws, often absurd, with which civilized man has tried to subdue the instinct throughout the centuries."

In the framework of the negotiation, Don Juan discovers himself by hiding and he hides when he is discovered. This behavior leads us to lock ourselves in falsehood and concealment of the true reasons. The tactic to overcome it is always to lead with clarity and transparency, within a framework of prudence and sagacity. As Jesus tells us in the book of Matthew (10:16), "Be wise as serpents and harmless as doves."

THE CHIEFTAIN OR SACKER

You have to pay attention to the thoughts that attack your weaknesses, so you know your weak side. It is our most vulnerable aspect, the one affected most often.

In the book of Luke (16: 1-12), Jesus Christ tells the parable of the shrewd manager.

"There was a rich man whose manager was accused of wasting his possessions. So he called him in and asked him, 'What is this I hear about you? Give an account of your management, because you cannot be manager any longer.' The manager said to himself, 'What shall I do now? My master is taking away my job. I'm not strong enough to dig, and I'm ashamed to beg— I know what I'll do so that, when I lose my job here, people will welcome me into their houses.' So he called in each one of his master's debtors. He asked the first, 'How much do you owe my master?' 'Nine hundred gallons of olive oil,' he replied. The manager told him, 'Take your bill, sit down quickly, and make it four hundred and fifty.' Then he asked the second, 'And how much do you owe?' 'A thousand bushels of wheat,' he replied. He told him, 'Take your bill and make it eight hundred.' The master commended the dishonest manager because he had acted shrewdly. For the people of this world are more shrewd in dealing with their own kind than are the people of the light. I tell you, use worldly wealth to gain friends for yourselves, so that when it is gone, you will be welcomed into eternal dwellings. Whoever can be trusted with very little can also be trusted with much, and whoever is dishonest with very little will also be dishonest with much. So if you have not been trustworthy in handling worldly wealth, who will trust you with true riches? And if you have not been trustworthy with someone else's property, who will give you property of your own?"

With this parable, Jesus did not invite us to cultivate deception or betrayal. Rather, he wanted to illustrate the importance of using the resources we have available for the good of others and to ensure our treasure is in heaven. If a corrupt manager knows how to manage his resources well, imagine what can be done by a fair and just person with a heart to serve others! Sometimes we think we do not have enough to give and to serve. You have to use creativity and open the mind to transcend, especially with justice.

THIRTEENTH RULE
Not everyone is a friend in the negotiation.

The enemy acts as someone that seduces and deceives a person who is already engaged to another; he seeks to maintain his provocations secretly so as not to be discovered. The enemy would tell us things like "Why are you going to say that if you will not be understood?" Therefore, the negotiator must turn to someone who really is going to help (a spiritual guide, an expert, a coach or a confessor) and not to someone who is going to consent (buddy or friend who is involved in the same process).

When I was working in the global corporate world, thanks to my performance, I quickly climbed the corporate ladder, and in less than a year, the company chose me to be enrolled in a program equivalent to an MBA on-the-job training. I was fortunate and blessed to learn key issues to examine, negotiate and sell projects at the executive level in leading world companies in various fields, from telecommunications, gas, petroleum, chemical and infrastructure to beverages and food

I got to know many managers in the course of the program. I remember a company vice president told me, "What a pity you wasted so much time studying master's, doctoral and even up to a post-doctoral degree! That's not important here." Listening to him, I was happy and sad. I was happy for me, because it was a sign that I was rising on the corporate ladder. When someone wants to minimize your work or your knowledge, these comments are part of a strategy of intimidation to demotivate you. I was saddened by the vice president. Just after hearing his comments, I thought, *Poor guy, he is afraid that I will take his job, but I'm not interested. If I was interested in any position, it would be the president's, not his.* In negotiations, whenever we meet this kind of enemy who does not want us to be successful because we overshadow them, we need to simply move on.

FOURTEENTH RULE
We must not lower our guard.

The enemy works as a thief, looking at what is the most vulnerable part of the house (our theological virtues, cardinal and moral) and never missing an opportunity to identify in which areas we are weak and needy. There is a door opening that helps him to come and steal. The temptation of the other is a warning for us to work on the areas where we are weakest.

Some try to prevent you from shining as a star in your life or in your career. That glow will come up even if they try to outshine you, and no worldly action will obscure or hinder your successes in the long run. I remember on one occasion that I negotiated one of the largest petrochemical projects that had ever been awarded to the company where I worked. Those who worked in business development for the company had an annual meeting where we presented projects with potential to be awarded globally in the company. Included on the list to be awarded was the petrochemical project I had sold and negotiated. At the last moment, the department manager asked me to cancel my trip, arguing that all others were to be at the event, and no one would stay in the office. I knew that he intended to draw me away from the spotlight and keep me from shining—to not give me the award and the place I had earned in the company. He was afraid that perhaps someone would steal his place. Such actions made me think about how important it is to get the most learning at all times.

Every day, every moment is a learning experience in life and we have the option to discern if we take it for better or for worse. As negotiators who transcend, we choose to take things for the good of it and make the best of ourselves in every situation, because that positive attitude will help us be better in the long term.

We must learn from the ancient civilizations, because their teachings are a warning to not make mistakes. They give us great tips to avoid big mistakes in life. The comparison table between making conventional decisions and decision-making for the Phoenicians that follows shows us the difference between being a negotiator that discerns for the short or long term.

These two extremes of decision-making styles can be used in different situations. The decision by the Phoenicians makes sense to transcend even a short-term negotiation. The most important highlight of the Phoenician decision versus a conventional viewpoint is that once the decision is made, there is no going back. If I make a commitment to a person, it is essential to keep my word in order not to pervert the purpose of the negotiation. A typical example, especially for lecturers, is when you are committed to a customer for a certain date, and a few days before the conference a conflict of agendas arises because another client, more strategic and of more importance, requests you for another conference for the same day. I know many speakers who have disappointed students at a university because they didn't keep their speaking engagement commitment but instead chose to visit a company. If from one moment to another, the speaker changes his initial commitment to the highest bidder, that wouldn't represent the Phoenician style.

Perhaps the revisable and reversible aspect of a conventional decision makes sense in the above example, as people try to minimize the cost and increase their position. It is arguable that in the short term, this kind of decision can increase their profits, but it is difficult to transcend this way.

Students, disappointed with the speaker who canceled to go with the company, could be potential customers of this speaker. It is very probable that these students will remember the incident and will not hire or give the speaker a good reference. There is a higher learning that emerges from all of this. In a negotiation, in order to transcend, we proceed in such a way that in the beginning, middle and end of the process, neither the intention with which it has begun nor the objective to be achieved will be perverted.

CONVENTIONAL DECISION	DECISION PHOENICIAN STYLE
Safe decision	Risky decision (not improvised or thoughtless)
At minimum cost	
Accurate and clear	The most cost
Revisable and reversible	Accurate, not entirely clear (Because of its complexity)
	Final and confident

SELF-FULFILLING PROPHECY

The self-fulfilling prophecy occurs when whatever we infer about a person becomes a reality, not because our inference is correct, but because our fearful or defensive action produces a similar reaction in the other. The inference causes us, rather than dealing with a person, to deal with a ghost that we have created of that person. That ghost interposes between the other and us. We imagine that the other has a personality that is not the true one, because it has been created by our own fantasy. The perception becomes reality and reality perception. This inferred reality creates separations and conflicts between people. Assumptions and unrealities dominate over the true reality. People become ghosts created by people, and the ghosts become people. So when two people are resolving a conflict between them, they are most likely acting and solving the problem between the two phantoms created from their inferences.

What to do? What is the solution to this situation? What do experts advise? Why do we sometimes act as irrational beings and manage conflict like wild beasts who fear being attacked (by the ghost created of the other)? Why do we not understand first what triggers this behavior in us, and then understand why the other acts in a similar way? What makes us build barriers rather than bridges of communication?

Think of a situation at work or in daily life that makes you feel frustration, anger, anguish, despair, helplessness, shame, disappointment, intimidation, anger, sadness—what must be the reason? What is the source of these feelings and emotions? Have you ever wondered if anything arises from an unmet and unsatisfied need of yours? Perhaps, when the other person is coming to ask you something, you use the meeting as a vehicle to vent your frustration (at what you have failed to solve in another area of your life), and download all your anger on the other. Would it not be productive to recognize that we have some unmet or unsatisfied need and put it aside for a moment to understand what the other needs at the time of making his petition?

Consider the situation methodically. First, ask yourself if the other side also shows his emotions. Why is that? Perhaps the premise is that emotions cloud our ability to think rationally and prevent us from reaching a decision, even if an amicable agreement is possible between the parties. So the hypothesis is that if we find the means to understand each other's needs, we will have fewer conflicts and increase the ability to meet our needs.

The key to understanding and meeting the needs of the other is to use integrative negotiation and a good communication process. Integrative negotiation, according to Harvard professors Ury and Fisher, consists of several elements: relationship, communication, posture, arguments, interest, options, reference or standard, legitimacy, the alternative to agreement and the agreement as such.

To build good communication between the parties, even if the ghosts in the conflict are well anchored, is to use a third party to mediate between the two conflicting ghosts. This third "neutral" party can use his gifts of discernment, temperance and fortitude to gradually dominate those ghosts and to make the parties realize and see the reality of the situation. For the neutral to understand the needs of both, it is suggested that he follow the footsteps of communication in third position or, in other words, the formula of asking, verifying, proposing and affirming. In doing so, the real needs of both parties will be explicit and he will be able to generate options that meet the needs that are a priority. Even in extreme cases, the ghosts of conflict may fade to let us see the real people. The biggest problem is when we transmit to others the ghost of another and create an unrealistic perception of someone. With no feedback, perception becomes reality, and the ghost becomes the person. If we use discernment, we avoid baseless talk and creating ghosts of others. This will be the first step toward understanding the other, giving the opportunity to speak and presenting him without being drawn into inferences.

CASE STUDY: THE JOURNEY OF WENAMEN

Acting on behalf of the Pharaoh Smendes, Wenamen was sent with linen, oils, and other goods valued in gold and silver (equivalent to five deben of gold and 31 deben of silver, a sum greater than an average Egyptian made in a lifetime) to purchase much-valued timber from Byblos for the Egyptian king. The sum he was willing to pay could have purchased many thousands of cords of wood. He arrived in this outpost of the former Egyptian empire only to be robbed, mistreated, and even imprisoned. In a well-known document referred to as The Report of Wenamen (written ca. 1570-1070 B.C.), a distressed Wenamen complains to the pharaoh about his misfortune and asks for more money.

He was sent to Byblos to buy wood for the sacred barque for Amon. He carried along a portable idol of Amon-of-the-Road. He landed in Dor and had his money stolen by a member of his crew. Wenamen blamed the local government. The King of Byblos, Zakar-Baals, refused to see him for twenty-nine days and finally one of the king's men had a frenzy of prophesying and demanded that they listen to Wenamen and his idol.
The Report of Wenamen, since its discovery in 1891, has been heralded as a literary masterpiece of the latter years of the New Kingdom and also as an illustration of the decay of Egypt's prestige abroad during this time period. As the Egyptian empire crumbled, something once as simple as trading for wood became quite difficult and Wenamen had

almost to plead with the King of Byblos to sell him the wood.

In the exchange of dialogues between Wenamen and the Phoenician King, we can see how the Phoenicians used principles and tools that have already discussed in the previous chapters. In this, the last section of our book, we are using the story of Wenamen as a case study to exemplify some concepts.

* * *

[13]
Here is his story by Herihor with the permission of Smendes I, prince of Tanis.
Year 5, fourth month of summer, day 16, the day of departure of Wenamun, the Elder of the Portal of the Temple of Amun, Lord of Thrones-of-the-Two-Lands, to fetch timber for the great noble bark of Amen-Re, King of Gods, which is upon the river and [is called] Amen-user-he.
On the day of my arrival at Tanis, the place where Smendes and Tentamun are, I gave them the dispatches of Amen-Re, King of Gods. They had read them out before them and they said: "I will do, I will do as Amen-Re, King of Gods, our lord has said."
I stayed until the fourth month of summer in Tanis. Then Smendes and Tentamun sent me off with the ship's captain Mengebet, and I went down upon the great sea of Phoenicia in the first month of summer, day 1. I arrived at Dor, a Tjeker town; and Beder, its prince, had fifty loaves, one jug of wine, and one ox-haunch brought to me. Then a man of my ship fled after stealing one vessel of gold worth 5 deben, four jars of silver worth 20 deben, and a bag with 11 deben of silver; [total of what he stole]: gold 5 deben, silver 31 deben.
That morning when I had risen, I went to where the prince was and said to him: "I have been robbed in your harbor. Now you are the prince of this land, you are the one who controls it. Search for my money! Indeed the money belongs to Amen-Re, King of Gods, the lord of the lands. It belongs to Smendes; it belongs to Herihor, my lord, and [to] the other

magnates of Egypt. It belongs to you; it belongs to Weret; it belongs to Mekmer; it belongs to Tjekerbaal, the prince of Byblos!" He said to me: "Are you serious? Are you joking? Indeed, I do not understand the demand you make to me. If it had been a thief belonging to my land who had gone down to your ship and had stolen your money, I would replace it for you from my storehouse, until your thief, whatever his name, had been found. But the thief who robbed you, he is yours, he belongs to your ship. Spend a few days here with me; I will search for him."
I stayed nine days moored in his harbor. Then I went to him and said to him: "Look, you have not found my money. [Let me depart] with the ship captains, with those who go to sea."

[The next eight lines are broken. Apparently the prince advises Wenamun to wait some more, but Wenamun departs. He passes Tyre and approaches Byblos. Then he seizes thirty deben of silver from a ship he has encountered which belongs to the Tjeker, an obvious act of piracy. He tells the owners that he will keep the money until his money has been found. Through this action he incurs the enmity of the Tjeker.]

They departed and I celebrated [in] a tent on the shore of the sea in the harbor of Byblos. And [I made a hiding place for] Amun-of-the-Road and placed possessions in it. Then the prince of Byblos sent to me saying: "[Leave my] harbor!" I sent to him, saying: "Where shall [I go]? ----------. If [you have a ship to carry me], let me be taken back to Egypt." I spent twenty-nine days in his harbor, and he spent time sending to me daily to say: "Leave my harbor!"
Now while he was offering to his gods, the god took hold of a young man [of] his young men and put him in a trance. He said to him: "Bring [the] god up! Bring the envoy who is carrying him! It is Amun who sent him. It is he who made him come!" Now it was while the entranced one was entranced that night that I had found a ship headed for Egypt. I had loaded all my belongings into it and was watching for the darkness, saying: "When it descends I will load the god so that no other eye shall see him."
Then the harbor master came to me, saying: "Wait until morning, says the prince!" I said to him: "Was it not you who daily took time to come to me, saying: 'Leave my harbor? Do you now say: 'Wait this night', in order to let the ship that I found depart, and then you will come to say: 'Go away'?" He went and told it to the prince. Then the prince sent to the captain of the ship, saying: "Wait until morning, says the prince."
When morning came, he sent and brought me up, while the god rested in the tent where he was on the shore of the sea. I found him seated in his

upper chamber with his back against a window, and the waves of the great sea of Phoenicia broke behind his head. I said to him: "Blessings of Amun!" He said to me: "How long is it to this day since you came from the place where Amun is?" I said to him: "Five whole months till now." He said to me: "If you are right, where is the dispatch of Amun that was in your hand? Where is the letter of the High Priest of Amun that was in your hand?" I said to him: "I gave them to Smendes and Tentamun." Then he became very angry and said to me: "Now then, dispatches, letters you have none. Where is the ship of pinewood that Smendes gave you? Where is its Phoenician crew? Did he not entrust you to this foreign ship's captain in order to have him kill you and have them throw you into the sea? From whom would one then seek the god? And you, from whom would one seek you?" So he said to me.

I said to him: "Is it not an Egyptian ship? Those who sail under Smendes are Egyptian crews. He has no Phoenician crews." He said to me: "Are there not twenty ships here in my harbor that do business with Smendes? As for Sidon, that other [place] you passed, are there not another fifty ships there that do business with Werekter and haul to this house?"

I was silent in this great moment. Then he spoke to me, saying: "On what business have you come?" I said to him: "I have come in quest of timber for the great noble bark of Amen-Re, King of Gods. What your father did, what the father of your father did, you too will do it." So I said to him. He said to me: "True, they did it. If you pay me for doing it, I will do it. My relations carried out this business after Pharaoh had sent six ships laden with the goods of Egypt, and they had been unloaded into their storehouses. You, what have you brought for me?"

[13] ANET 25-29

We could infer from the text that the Egyptian priest does not generate confidence and credibility with the Phoenician monarch, who refuses to receive him, and the context in which the Egyptian was immersed. During his first meeting, the Phoenician monarch poses the relevant questions to generate the necessary confidence. We could debate that the king of Byblos is using the gift of **discernment** to ask all those questions and, to some extent, a degree of prudence to understand what Wenamen needed and what his mission was. In the following dialogue we will see how the Phoenician monarch uses **fortitude** and **temperance** to not bow before the priest sent by the pharaoh.

He had the daybook of his forefathers brought and had it read before me. They found entered in his book a thousand deben of silver and all sorts of things. He said to me: "If the ruler of Egypt were the lord of what is mine and I were his servant, he would not have sent silver and gold to say: 'Carry out the business of Amun.' It was not a royal gift that they gave to my father! I too I am not your servant, nor am I the servant of him who sent you! If I shout aloud to the Lebanon, the sky opens and the logs lie here on the shore of the sea! Give me the sails you brought to move your ships, loaded with logs for [Egypt]! Give me the ropes you brought [to lash the pines] that I am to fell in order to make them for you ----, -------------- that I am to make for you for the sails of your ships; or the yards may be too heavy and break, and you may die [in] the midst of the sea. For Amun makes thunder in the sky ever since he placed Seth beside him! Indeed, Amun has founded all the lands. He founded them after having first founded the land of Egypt from which you have come. Thus craftsmanship came from it in order to reach the place where I am! Thus learning came from it in order to reach the place where I am! What are these foolish travels they made you do?"
I said to him: "Wrong! These are not foolish travels that I am doing. There is no ship on the river that does not belong to Amun. His is the sea and his the Lebanon of which you say, 'It is mine.' It is a growing

ground for Amen-user-he, the lord of every ship. Truly, it was Amen-Re, King of Gods, who said to Herihor, my master: 'Send me!' And he made me come with this great god. But look, you have let this great god spend these twenty-nine days moored in your harbor. Did you not know that he was here? Is he not he who he was? You are prepared to haggle over the Lebanon with Amun, its lord? As to your saying the former kings sent silver and gold: If they had owned life and health, they would not have sent these things. It was in place of life and health that they sent these things to your fathers! But Amen-Re, King of Gods, he is the lord of life and health, and he was the lord of your fathers! They passed their lifetimes offering to Amun. You too, you are the servant of Amun!

If you will say 'I will do' to Amun, and will carry out his business, you will live, you will prosper, you will be healthy; you will be beneficent to your whole land and your people. Do not desire what belongs to Amun-Re, King of Gods! Indeed, a lion loves his possessions! Have your scribe brought to me that I may send him to Smendes and Tentamun, the pillars Amun has set up for the north of his land; and they will send all that is needed. I will send him to them, saying 'Have it brought until I return to the south; then I shall refund you all your expenses.'" So I said to him.

Here we observe that the Egyptian priest brought the negotiations to a more spiritual level. The Phoenician monarchs, apart from being good negotiators, were very religious. By appealing to the power of the king of the gods, he convinced the Phoenician monarch to send a messenger to Egypt.

He placed my letter in the hand of his messenger; and he loaded the keel, the prow-piece, and the stern-piece, together with four other hewn logs, seven in all, and sent them to Egypt. His messenger who had gone to Egypt returned to me in Phoenicia in the first month of winter, Smendes and Tentamun having sent: four jars and one kakmen-vessel of gold; five jars of silver; ten garments of royal linen; ten hrd-garments of fine linen; five hundred smooth linen maats; five hundred ox-hides; five hundred ropes; twenty sacks of lentils; and thirty baskets of fish. And she sent to me: five garments of fine linen; five hrd-garments of fine linen; one sack of lentils; and five baskets of fish.

The prince rejoiced. He assigned three hundred men and three hundred oxen, and he set supervisors over them to have them fell the timbers. They were felled and they lay there during the winter. In the third month of

summer they dragged them to the shore of the sea. The prince came out and stood by them, and he sent to me saying: "Come!" Now when I had been brought into his presence, the shadow of his sunshade fell on me. Then Penamun, a butler of his, intervened, saying: "The shadow of Pharaoh, your lord, has fallen upon you." And he was angry with him and said: "Leave him alone."
As I stood before him, he addressed me, saying: "Look, the business my fathers did in the past, I have done it, although you did not do for me what your fathers did for mine. Look, the last of your timber has arrived and is ready. Do as I wish, and come to load it. For has it not been given to you? Do not come to look at the terror of the sea. For if you look at the terror of the sea, you will see my own! Indeed, I have not done to you what was done to the envoys of Khaemwese, after they had spent seventeen years in this land. They died on the spot." And he said to his butler: "Take him to see the tomb where they lie."
I said to him: "Do not make me see it. As for Khaemwese, the envoys he sent you were men and he himself was a man. You have not here one of his envoys, though you say: 'Go and see your companions.' Should you not rejoice and have a stela [made] for yourself, and say on it: 'Amen-Re, King of Gods, sent me Amun-of-the-Road, his envoy, together with Wenamun, his human envoy, in quest of timber for the great noble bark of Amen-Re, King of Gods. I felled it; I loaded it; I supplied my ships and my crews. I let them reach Egypt so as to beg for me from Amun fifty years of life over and above my allotted fate.' And if it comes to pass that in another day an envoy comes from the land of Egypt who knows writing and he reads out your name on the stela, you will receive water of the west like the gods who are there."
He said to me: "A great speech of admonition is what you have said to me." I said to him: "As to the many [things] you have said to me; if I reach the place where the High Priest of Amun is and he sees your accomplishment, it is your accomplishment that will draw profit to you."

In the above passage, the Egyptian priest has negotiated with the Phoenician king in a religious and spiritual dimension. We can infer that the Phoenician enjoyed this conversation, because he says what Wenamen just said is good advice.

I went off to the shore of the sea, to where the logs were lying. And I saw eleven ships that had come in from the sea and belonged to the Tjeker

[who were] saying: "Arrest him! Let no ship of his leave for the land of Egypt!" Then I sat down and wept. And the secretary of the prince came out to me and said to me: "What is it?" I said to him: "Do you not see the migrant birds going down to Egypt a second time? Look at them traveling to the cool water! Until when shall I be left here? For do you not see those who have come to arrest me?"
He went and told it to the prince. And the prince began to weep on account of the words said to him, for they were painful. He sent his secretary out to me, bringing two jugs of wine and a sheep. And he sent me Tentne, an Egyptian songstress who was with him, saying: "Sing for him! Do not let his heart be anxious." And he sent to me, saying: "Eat, drink; do not let your heart be anxious. You shall hear what I will say tomorrow."

In this dialogue, we can clearly see the sense of *Tradeables* offered by the Phoenician monarch to Wenamen. The monarch makes every effort to make sure Wenamen feels good. He is sad and desolate, but the Phoenician sends him a singer to have a good time.

When morning came, he had his assembly summoned. He stood in their midst and said to the Tjeker: "What have you come for?" They said to him: "We have come after the blasted ships that you are sending to Egypt with our enemy." He said to them: "I cannot arrest the envoy of Amun in my country. Let me send him off, and you go after him to arrest him."

The Phoenician monarch behaves before the Tjeker in a very **just** and **prudent** manner, and, in conclusion, he convinces them to let Wenamen go.

He had me board and sent off from the harbor of the sea. And the wind drove me to the land of Alasiya. Then the town's people came out against me to kill me. But I forced my way through them to where Hatiba, the princess of the town, was. I met her coming from one of her houses to enter another. I saluted her and said to the people who stood around her: "Is there not one among you who understands Egyptian?" And one among them said: "I understand it." I said to him: "Tell my lady that I have heard it said as far away as Thebes, the place where Amun is: 'If wrong is done in every town, in the land of Alasiya right is done.' Now is wrong done here too every day?"
She said: "What is it you have said?" I said to her: "If the sea rages and the wind drives me to the land where you are, will you let me be received so as to kill me, though I am the envoy of Amun? Look, as for me, they would search for me till the end of time. As for this crew of the prince of Byblos, whom they seek to kill, will not their lord find ten crews of yours and kill them also?" She had the people summoned and they were reprimanded. She said to me: "Spend the night - the story is broken here

The story ends here, but it is likely that Wenamen has returned to Egypt, because if he had not, there would be no testimony of his journey.

CHAPTERS SUMMARY

In the first chapter, **Negotiate with faith**, we learned that from the silence we can find fulfillment, and in the dark, opportunity. In addition to introducing the concept of transgenerational negotiation, we reviewed the notions of negotiation with meaning, identity and creating desert to motivate the search for better solutions and enhance our capabilities to be and to transcend. We also analyze barter and Phoenician heritage as basic tools that help us go beyond transactional. We review how to incorporate the notion of common good to the transcendental negotiation and the need to answer the two key questions for this book: how to transcend and, if possible, transcend from faith. We conclude that it is possible only if we build our relationships on the pillars of ethics. To find the meaning of negotiation and not lose ourselves on the road, it is advisable to act from a linear view of history, as this allows us to interpret events as opportunities to build. In the following chapters we analyzed, one by one, the main virtues and their effect on the transcendental negotiation. We begin in Chapter II with **prudence**, the exercise of an inner strength that implies knowing ourselves. We study the collaborative negotiation from our experience with youth in Guatemala, committed to exercise good in their daily lives. We explore the concepts of integrative bargaining and *Tradeables*, a technique based on the philosophy of giving, which places prudence in the center of the actions of a negotiator. To do this, we use the Johari Window, a tool that allows us to analyze and classify customer

260

needs. We did the same with the negotiator role of the donor and the different emotions that are generated in the client when their needs are met. This helped us to understand the deep connection and loyalty bond between customer and supplier. We contrast these categories with the scale of satisfaction proposed by Lopez Quintas, in which we can see the satisfaction of a need is directly proportional to the depth of the bond between people. For example, at level 2 of the Lopez Quintas scale, the negotiated object carries meaning, purpose and value greater than the same non-negotiated object; from the point of view of *Tradeables,* this is equivalent to giving transcendental value to objects as symbols of a relationship. In short, generating *Tradeables* sets us on the path of a transcendental negotiation. Thus, we conclude that a negotiation can become reckless, reactive or impulsive as one responds to blind instinct and passions.

In Chapter III, we define what **justice** is and how we can transcend from this virtue. We also explore what characterizes justice with regard to prudence. **Prudence** is dedicated to perfecting the "I" advising what is good for oneself. **Justice**, however, has the task of generating order in anything that puts us in relationship with others. A person is just to the extent that he recognizes the otherness (the difference and the identity of the other) and seeks to give everyone correspondingly. We learned that justice as human virtue resides ultimately in an inner motivating force rather than in a desire for power. This means that in real negotiation, to be just, you do not need the *potestas* (power), rather, you need the *autoritas* (authority). In addressing the issue of social justice, we analyzed the paradox of an injustice which we believe to be fair and vice versa. For those who do not believe in a transcendent entity, justice is relative; for those who do, justice is absolute. After all, this situation is like the negotiating dilemma. Do I collaborate or compete; am I right or wrong?

In Chapter IV, we analyze **fortitude** and show some ways to transform inner strength and vulnerability to transcend in the negotiation. First, to be strong means to act justly, since strength without justice becomes a lever for evil. We also analyze how to combat anger and fear in the negotiation, and for that we turn to Thomas Kilmann's five conflict management styles. We confirm that **fortitude** is not the result of going through difficulties or heavy efforts, but generates good for everyone. From that idea, we review the relationship between gratitude, gratuitousness and fortitude. Finally, we explore the psychic strength and resilience essential for every human being who wants to transcend.

Temperance, the subject of the fifth chapter, is the virtue that defends and saves Self to be protected from Oneself, as in human nurture there's a tendency to go against one's own nature. We must recover the deep and anthropological sense of this virtue, especially when incorporated in such a *sui generis (*unique from Latin*)* field as negotiation, where tension and conflict prevail. We learned that a moderate person owns himself.

Passions do not have superiority over reasoning, will and heart. That is the fundamental and radical value of the virtue of **temperance**, indispensable for human beings to reach fullness. In negotiation situations, we need to integrate the emotional and cultural dimensions to avoid falling into misunderstandings. **Temperance** is a virtue that integrates all the faculties of the human being in a harmonious way, and to illustrate this, we shared the story of my two eternal loves, the cities of Cadiz and Puerto Vallarta. I learned by experience to practice **temperance** to negotiate a great project, moderating voluntarism and objectively reaching solutions that satisfy most of those involved.

In the last chapter, we talked about **discernment**. This helps us to refine the distinction of what appears to have the same value but, in fact, does not.

In this chapter, we describe steps to make educated choices with transcendent meaning. We also analyze the story of a Cherokee chief, the three thoughts of ancient historians, and the Freudian triad to explore the spiritual dimension (soul or psyche) of the human being. All three stories coincide in one respect: one of the ways in which the spiritual dimension is manifested is through discernment. Without it, we would be unable to distinguish what brings us closer or farther away from transcendence. We also proposed a daily thermometer of negotiation based on the psychological tools of resonance and dissonance. The resonance, within the context of this work, means to perceive intuitively if the concepts presented here echo within us from the spiritual point, and not so much from the intellect. Dissonance is the lack of conformity or proportion which some things must naturally have. Finally, we present two useful references, the fourteen rules for dealing with faith and the story of *Wenamen*, the Egyptian priest, as a case study to illustrate some concepts of the book.

GENERAL CONCLUSION

To achieve transcendental negotiations, the human being must surpass himself and think about the impact his negotiations will have on future generations. Given the great development problems being experienced by humanity, we sometimes experience anxiety and depression. The word of God encourages us: "*I am with you always, to the very end of the age*" (Mt 28: 20). An open and transcendent humanism can guide us to make forms of social and civil life at all levels: structures, institutions, culture and so on. The main driving force behind authentic development is charity (from *caritas*, love), an extraordinary momentum that moves us to commit ourselves with courage and generosity in relationships where justice and peace prevail. It is a force that has its origin in God. Even four thousand years ago, this was very well known by the Phoenicians, whom we recognize even today as the best negotiators in history. Their prosperity of trade was due to their thankfulness to their gods, manifested in their temples built in all parts of the Mediterranean, conquered commercially and peacefully. We could infer that a divine relationship is what made the Phoenician civilization act in a transcendental way. Defending the truth, to articulate it with humility and conviction, and to witness to it in life are therefore exacting and indispensable forms of the loving impulse that lives in the mind and heart of every human being— that source that reveals our transcendental mission.

When we act with the truth, we listen carefully and avoid falling into the cultural and historical determinations and appreciate the value of people and things. We are thinking, feeling and acting. One way to open up to transcendence, not only in every relationship but in every negotiation, is to implement the tools and values that we propose in this book, not only for its potential commercial interaction, but for the alternatives that we provide for conflict management present in our daily lives. These are inevitable. It is, therefore, important to manage them with integrity, placing discernment, prudence, justice, fortitude and temperance as the spine that is not subject to conventions of the day, but fundamentals of the first order. From ancient civilizations, we have learned not only to be wise, strong, temperate and just, but also to be grateful and sagacious. These are necessary conditions to achieve high performance in the negotiation process. These learnings propel us toward an open future. This is why this book, rather than giving us answers for the road to follow, encourages us to reflect upon an essential question from start to finish: *Quo vadis*—where are you going, negotiator? The answer provides direction and meaning and will reveal our quality as negotiators and transcendental human beings. Negotiating is the opposite of manipulation, to take abusive advantage and unilateral benefits. Only by knowing the other side from the human dimension, respecting his dignity, speaking the truth and honoring agreements, can we reach transcendence as the Phoenicians, the best negotiators in history, did.

WHAT THE EXPERTS ARE SAYING

Habib Chamoun has done a remarkable job of creating insights into the 'soul' of negotiation, combining perspectives on anthropology, ethics and theology into a new perspective he calls 'transcendental negotiation'. Readers will find a refreshing perspective on negotiation, not just as technique, but as a way of leading a virtuous life.

Dr. Roy Lewicki
Abramowitz Professor of Management
and Human Resources Emeritus,
Max M. Fisher College of Business
The Ohio State University

Habib Chamoun provides a glimpse into the mind of the transcendent negotiator: prudence, justice, temperance, fortitude and discernment play important roles. Since every human interaction implies the possibility of negotiation, he urges us to transcend the transactional, offering an appealing meditation on elements of negotiation practice that are too often overlooked.

Dr. Larry Susskind
MIT Professor and Co-Founder
Program on Negotiation at Harvard Law School

Every time you negotiate, you define your values. Yes, you seek to advance your own interests—or those of the individuals and organizations you represent. But all the actions you undertake—everything that you do and say—also establish your character.

But what (if anything) do you owe the people across the table with whom you negotiate? Must you always be fair? Do you have to be honest? More fundamentally, what is fairness and honesty in negotiation?

Dr. Habib Chamoun-Nicolás's bold and inspiring book *Transcend!* addresses these challenging questions with wisdom drawn from his own impressive experience and scholarship. He explains how success in negotiation (and in life more generally) requires prudence, justice, fortitude, temperance, and discernment. His groundbreaking book deserves a place of honor on every serious negotiator's bookshelf.

Dr. Michael Wheeler MBA Class of 1952 and Professor of Management Practice
Harvard Business School, Soldiers Field of Boston, Massachusetts

Dr. Habib Chamoun-Nicolas has once more performed in this book a truly impressive work. He not only surprises us with his superb and enjoyable style of writing that once you start reading, it is impossible to put down, but also by his profound knowledge of very diverse situations on the subject of negotiation and his very assertive approach to historical recollections. A book written from wisdom, intelligence, joy and kindness. A fascinating reading even for laymen on the subject, as in my case.

Dr. Carlos G. Wagner President of CEFYP
(Center of Phoenician and Punic Studies)
Universidad Complutense
Madrid, Spain

In his previous book *Negotiate Like a Phoenician*, Professor Habib Chamoun-Nicolas explains how the Phoenicians were known to have been the most successful traders among ancient civilizations thanks to their negotiating skills and methodology. Phoenicians were famous for many inventions, especially for their success in international commerce, and for being the fathers of one of the first successful globalization experiences in history, peacefully becoming the dominant commercial power in the Mediterranean region and far beyond.

Professor Chamoun-Nicolas is an expert in international negotiations and in the Phoenician trade history. In his new book *Transcend!* Professor Chamoun-Nicolas delves into an anthropological aspect of successful negotiators where character is of utmost importance. He dissects the negotiation process and discusses how a negotiator's character influences negotiations, citing honesty, integrity and justice as the basis for long-term successful negotiations, such as in the international diplomacy arena. *Transcend!* is a must-read for anyone who wants to be a successful negotiator.

*Massoud Maalouf, Former
Ambassador of Lebanon to Canada, Poland and Chile.*

As usual, Dr. Habib Chamoun Nicolas has provided an extraordinary work on negotiation. This new contribution to the discipline will surely serve all the public: researchers, diplomats, students, experts and practitioners. This brilliantly written book is easy to read and invites the reader who is interested in negotiating to know oneself and learn about each other in order to carry out together a win-win negotiation.

Dr. Doudou Sidibé
Scientific Coordinator
International Biennale on Negotiation
Novancia Business School of Paris
France

Dr. Habib Chamoun-Nicolas and his collaborators offer in *Transcend!* an ethical way of functioning not only for negotiators, but also for those in any leadership position. The ancient Cardinal Virtues of Justice, Prudence, Temperance, and Fortitude provide the lens through which discerned action occurs that moves beyond the transactional toward the transcendental. *Transcend!* imparts a vision of collaboration that is co-responsible and will help leaders, including those of religious congregations, be more effective in their functioning.

Very Rev. Frank Donio, S.A.C., D.Min.
Director
Catholic Apostolate Center
Washington, D.C.

Habib writes in a friendly tone, just as he teaches his courses and workshops, and splashes his work with anecdotes captivating the reader and immersing him into it to discover and enjoy the depth of the writings. *Transcend! Quo Vadis Negotiator* presents us with a scheme that goes beyond the win-win. He mentions that if you want to have a negotiation that will endure long term, as did the Phoenicians more than two thousand years, it must be done ethically and in accordance with natural law. Just as important as the result is the way to reach to it. We must know how to discern and exercise the virtues of prudence, justice, fortitude and temperance, opposing the ego, hypocrisy, arrogance and envy. Chamoun-Nicolas shows us that trust and active listening are important, while distrust and intrigue are cancers of negotiation. The book reminds us that the person is worthy for what he is, and not for what he has nor for what he does. Being a good negotiator is to connect with yourself and to find out the meaning of your actions. Every human relationship involves a negotiation, therefore I consider *Transcend! Quo Vadis Negotiator* essential reading.

Antonio Sánchez Díaz de Rivera
Vice President
UPAEP University, Puebla, Mexico

Dr. Chamoun's book *Transcend! Quo Vadis Negotiator* is written in a deep and profound humanistic and spiritual style. The great experiences inside the book are entertaining and funny, making the readers to connect and to look back at the stories. · The business-based success stories are the heart in *Transcend! Quo Vadis Negotiator,* with the author succeeding to open first with the cardinal virtues to make it wide and transcendental.

Prof. P. Dr. Karl Josef Wallner
Rector of the Philosophy and Theology
Benedict XVI Pontifical University
Holy Cross Cistercian Monastery,
Heiligenkreuz, Austria

This book offers an anthropological perspective on negotiation, focusing on the important moral dimension of negotiators. Incorporating examples from historical and religious texts, along with anecdotes from his own life, Chamoun-Nicolas draws readers into his reflections on negotiation through the ages as he highlights the ethical principles of a successful negotiator.

Audrey Tetteh, Education
Program Director
ICONS Project
University of Maryland

This book is really powerful because it has the power of witness of life and consistency of the author. It also is powerful because it will make you take a break from your busy life to reflect on what we need to learn or strengthen in our lives to achieve our negotiating objectives.

I am certain that if we strive to apply what the author proposes with his close, wise and anecdotal style, we will be better human beings, excellent negotiators and certainly more integral and happy people. Negotiations will then be a tool and not a purpose in themselves.

I invite you to read this text with great conviction that this will not be just another book, and surely his teachings will accompany us the rest of our lives.

Josefina Vázquez Mota
First Woman Candidate by a Majority Party to the Mexican Presidency

With clear and simple manner; with theoretical and theological support; with anecdotes, stories and examples; giving us recommendations and methodologies, and inviting us to self-assess, we discover how these precepts help us in our relationships and in our daily interaction with other human beings to achieve what we are looking for.

I would summarize *Transcend!* in the following sentence: To be great negotiators we have to go back to the origin.

Transcend! is a must-read for all.

I conclude with this sentence from the text itself: "Discernment, prudence, justice, fortitude and temperance are the backbone of a trade or activity not subject to conventions of the day, but anthropological foundations of the first order."

David Noel Ramírez
Former Dean of Monterrey TEC

I have always believed that any change starts within; what is surrounding us is a reflection of what we think, say, do and fail to do. Everything has an impact on our environment, hence the importance of considering what the book *Transcend!* reminds us not only to achieve successful negotiations, but above all to be happier: the importance of learning to discern and choose correctly, be aware that we are what we repeatedly do, and the possibility of becoming extraordinary people depending on our choice. For me, freedom is the master key to all our possibilities and all our creations. The challenge is to understand that freedom and responsibility are two sides of the same coin. To be free and choose correctly, it is imperative that we are responsible for our words and actions. As stated in these pages, the first responsibility we must assume is to know ourselves to meet our own self, our essence, then connect with others and achieve prosperity. In the end, the only way to transcend is to distinguish between what feeds the ephemeral and what helps to build the eternal. We learned that where our treasure is, there is our heart. Let us not miss the opportunity to live intensely every day with great passion, transmitting that enthusiasm to everyone we meet on the road, whether in negotiations or in another context. Truth, love and defending freedom is the calling that we all share. Let us make the right decisions; we are still on time.

Armando Regil Velasco
President
IPEA

Daily life is a continuous act of negotiating, at home, in the office, while shopping or in public life. There are those who have not developed this ability to negotiate, and not all the ways to negotiate are the same. In today's society, dominated by increasingly sophisticated forms of selfishness, you think about wanting to negotiate only with the objective to optimize the personal benefit, which ends up in increasingly poor human relations, where there is mistrust, abuse or indifference.

The great merit of this book is precisely that the author invites us to transcend in the negotiation. Contemporary society needs women and men who are great negotiators, who know how to manage the great values of justice, solidarity, truth or beauty, not encountering any objection to do good, do well, and always do the best possible. There are many frustrated lives living in deprivation, bitterness, sadness or loneliness for not knowing how to cultivate the art of negotiation, to transcend inside and outside the family, not wanting to demonstrate in practice the human capacity to seek happiness in the good of others, in order to experience an "I love you, I want your good, I want the best for you."
In its pages of history and illustrative and entertaining anecdotes, *Transcends! Quo Vadis Negotiator* makes the ideal of virtue and the good life, reminding us what it takes to build the civilization of love.

Dr. Guillermo Cantú
Researcher Professor
Panamericana University
México, D.F.

BIBLIOGRAPHY

ADLER, N. J. *Negotiating with Foreigners. Society Culture and Management.* Berlin, T. D. Weinshall, Walter de Gruyter & Co, 1993, 501-535.

ADLER, A. *Problems of neurosis: A book of case histories.* P. Mairet, Ed., New York: Harper & Row, 1964.

AFIFI Soweid, Rema A, El Kak, F, Major, S. C, Karam, D. K, Rouhana A. Changes in health-related attitude and self-reported behavior of undergraduate students at the American University of Beirut following a health awareness course. *Education for Health: Change in Learning & Practice.* Taylor & Francis Ltd., Vol. 16 Issue 3, Nov. 2003, 265.

ANDREW M. Kaikati, and Jack G. Kaikati. "Business Insight (A Special Report): Pricing --- Let's make a deal: The growing role of barter in the marketplace", *Wall Street Journal.* Eastern edition, 2010.

ANTONIONI, D. *Relationship between the big five personality factors and conflict management style.* Int J Confl Manag. 1998; 9(4):336-55.

AQUINAS, St. Thomas. 1271. *Summa theologica.* Calvin College: Christian Classics Ethereal Library, Part II, Question 26, Article 4. Available at http://www.ccel.org/browse/bookInfo?id=aquinas/summa (última consulta, Marzo 29, 2009).

BARRETO, L. *The role of ontological coaching on assuring quality: An approach for the professional competencies of the employees.* Master Thesis, UAT, México, 2009.

BASTON, C. D., B. Duncan, P. Ackerman, T. Buckley, and K. Birch. "Is empathic emotion a source of altruistic motivation", *Journal of Personality and Social Psychology,* 40(2), 1981, 290-302.

BENET-MARTÍNEZ, V and Shigehiro, Oishi. *Culture and Personality.* To appear in O.P. John, R.W. Robins, & L.A. Pervin (Editors), *Handbook of Personality: Theory and Research.* Gilford Press, 2006.

BERGER, W. G. *Some correlates of attitude change, retention of attitude related material, and evaluation of the communicator.* Ph.D. dissertation, Michigan State University, 1969.

BILLING, O, Gillin, D, and Davidson, W. "Aspects of personality and culture in a Guatemalan Community: Ethnological and Rorschach approaches", *Journal of Personality*. Dec 47, Vol. 16, Issue 2, p 153-187.

BOELE, D. R., and Marco, P. *Big Five assessment*, Hogrefe & Huber, Seattle, 2002.

BROCKMAN, J, Nunez, A, and Basu, A. "Effectiveness of a conflict resolution training program in changing graduate students style of managing conflict with their faculty advisors", *Innovative Higher Education*, Vol. 35 Issue 4, August 2010, 277-293.

Catecismo de la iglesia católica, 2nd edition, Madrid: Librería Editrice Vaticana, 2001.

CAPLAN, L. *The good advocate.* Legal Affairs (May-June), 2004. Disponible en: http://www.legalaffairs.org/issues/May-June-2004/editorial_mayjun04.msp (last accessed Mar. 29, 2009).

CARRELL, M., M. Shank, and J. Barbero. "Fairness norms in negotiation: A Study of American and European perspectives", *Dispute Resolution Journal*, 64.1, 2009, 54-60.

CHAMOUN, H. and HAZLETT, R. "The psychology of giving and its effect on negotiation", *Rethinking Negotiation Teaching Series: Innovations for Context and Culture*, edited by C. Honeyman, J. Coben, and G. DePalo, St. Paul, MN: DRI Press, 2009.

_____ *Negotiate like a Phoenician*, Houston: Key-Negotiations, 2007.

_____ "The influence of emotions in negotiation: A game theory framework: Educating negotiators in a connected world", *Rethinking Negotiation Teaching Series, Vol 4*. Edited by C. Honeyman, J. Coben, and A. Wei Min Lee. St. Paul, MN: DRI Press.

_____ _____, Matta Vega, A.I. "A journey towards negotiation behavioral change", *Avoiding and Competing to Collaborate*, presented at the 5th edition of the International Biennial of Negotiation at Novancia Business School of Paris, Paris, France, 2014.

_____ _____, Valderrey, Fco, and Chiu, J.S.P. "Bartering: When negotiations need a creative approach."

Vol.2. Issue 1, July 2014, TANPAN Chinese-American Journal on Negotiations, Hong Kong.

_____, Fuller, B, Benitez, D, "Bringing the street to the classroom and the student to the street: Guided forays into street-wise negotiations. Educating negotiators in a connected world", *Rethinking Negotiation Teaching Series*, Vol 4. Edited by C. Honeyman, J. Coben, and A. Wei Min Lee. St. Paul, MN: DRI Press, 2013.

CHARLES, T. *Ética de la Autenticidad*, Barcelona, Paidós, 1994.

CIALDINI, R. B. *Influence: Science and Practice*. 4th edition, Boston, MA: Allyn and Bacon, 2001.

_____, *Influence: The psychology of persuasion*. New York: William Morrow, 1993.

COHN, Laura. "What you need to know about bartering", *Kiplinger's Personal Finance*, 63.10, 2009, 79.

COSTA, P. T., Jr. and R. M. McCrae. *Revised NEO Personality Inventory [NEO-PI-R] and Five Factor Inventory [NEO-FFI] Professional Manual*. Odessa, FL: Psychological Assessment Resources, Inc, 1992.

CURALL, S.C. and Inkpen, A.C. "A multilevel approach to trust in joint ventures", *Journal of International Business Studies*. Washington D.C., 33.3, Third Quarter, 2002, 479-495.

DAHL, Darren. *A new kind of barter system*. Inc. 32.4, 2010, 112-114.

DANIELS, V. *International Sales: How to Excel in Global Selling* (Disc., 2004)

Diccionario Larousse: Pequeño Larousse ilustrado, Colombia: Larousse, 2000.

DRUCKMAN, Daniel, William Zartman and J. Lewis Rasmussen. "Negotiating in the International Context", *Peacemaking in international conflict: Methods & techniques*, Washington, D.C.: Institute of Peace, 1982.

Estelas en el aire, palabras sobre el mar: Wenamón y el monarca fenicio, Gerión, 26, 1, 2008, 23-34.

EDITORIAL Committee. *Chinese civilization: A sourcebook*. City University of Hong Kong Press: Revised Edition, 2000.

ELAINE, Allison. *Understanding how personalities affect negotiations*. American Agent & Broker, 2006.

ELÍADE, Mircea. *El mito del eterno retorno*, Madrid: Alianza/Emecé, 2002.

FESBACH, N. D. 'Empathy, the formative years: Implications for clinical practice, *Empathy Reconsidered: New Directions in Psychotherapy*. A. C. Bohart and L. S. Greenberg, Washington DC: American Psychological Association, 1997, 33-59.

FILZMOSER M. and R. Vetschera. "A classification of bargaining steps and their impact on negotiation outcomes", *Group Decision and Negotiation*. 17.5, 2008, 421-443.

FISHER R., Ury W. &Patton, B. *Getting to yes, 3rd Edition.* New York: Penguin Books, 2001.

FOSTER, D.A. *Bargaining across borders: How to negotiate business successfully anywhere in the world*. New York, NY: McGraw Hill, 1992.

FORSYTHE, R. S. *Assumed similarity and accuracy in observing people,* Master's thesis, Michigan State University, 1970.

FRANCISCO, Pope. *Enciclica "Laudato Si'*, Rome, Italy, 2015.
FRANKL, Viktor, and Winslade, W. *Man's search for meaning*. Beacon Press, 2006.

FREUD, Sigmund. *An autobiographical study. The standard edition of the complete psychological works of Sigmund Freud*. Trans. and ed. James Strachey. Vol. 20. London: Hogarth, 1959. 1–74. 24 vols. 1953–74.

FULMER, I., B. Barry, and D. Long. "Lying and smiling: Informational and emotional deception in negotiation", *Journal of Business Ethics*, 88.4, 2009, 691-709.

GEERT Hofstede. *Culture's consequences: Comparing values, behaviors, institutions and organization across nations*. 2nd ed, Newbury Park, CA: Sage, 2003.

GERSHMAN, Michael. "The basics of barter", *Management Review*, 75.11, 1986, 49.

GESTELAND, R.R. *Cross-cultural business behavior: Marketing, Negotiating and managing across cultures*. Copenhagen, Denmark: Copenhagen Business School Press, 1999.

GOEDICKE, H. *The report of Wenamun*, Baltimore: Johns Hopkins University Press, 1975.

GOH, B.C, Chamoun, H, Deason, F, Folberg, J, and Sukhsimranjit, S. "As we see it: Educating negotiators in a connected world", *Rethinking Negotiation Teaching Series, vol 4*, edited by C. Honeyman, J. Coben, and A. Wei Min Lee. St. Paul, MN: DRI Press.

GOLDBERG, L. R. *The development of markers for the Big Five factor structure*, Psychol. Assess., 4(1), 1992, 26–42.

HAMPDEN-Turner, C.M. and Trompenaars, F., *Building cross-cultural competence: How to create wealth from conflicting values*. New Haven, CT: Yale University Press, 2000.

HARNICK, Fieke and Naomi Ellemers. "Hide and seek: The effects of revealing one's personal interests in intra- and intergroup negotiations", *European Journal of Social Psychology*, 36.6, 2006, 791-813.

HARRIS, P.R. and Moran, R.T. *Managing cultural differences*. Houston, TX: Gulf Publishing, 5th Ed., 1996.

HERODOTUS. *The Histories*, transl. George Rawlinson, New York: Alfred A. Knopf, 1997.

HOFFMAN, K.S. and Dalin, S. D. *The Art of barter: How to trade for almost anything*. Skyhorse Publishing, New York, NY, 2010.

HOFSTEDE, G. *Cultures and organizations*. London: McGraw-Hill, 1991.

HOLST, Sanford. *Phoenicians: Lebanon's epic heritage*. Los Angeles, CA: Cambridge and Boston Press, 2005.

HURN, Brian J. "The influence of culture on international business negotiations", *Industrial and Commercial Training* 39.7, 2007, 354.

JOHN, O. P. and Srivastava, S. "The Big Five trait taxonomy: History, measurement, and theoretical perspectives." *Handbook of personality: Theory and research*, L. A. Pervin and O. P. John, eds., Guilford, New York, 1999.

JOHNSTON, T. *Did the Phoenicians discover America?* Houston: St. Thomas Press, 1965.

JORDAN, J. "Relational development through mutual empathy." In *Empathy reconsidered: New directions in psychotherapy*, edited by A. C. Bohart and L. S. Greenberg, Washington, DC: American Psychological Association, 1997.

JUNG, C.G. *The relations between the ego and the unconscious. CW 7,* (1934 [1953]).

KAIKATI, Jack G. "The Reincarnation of barter trade as a marketing tool", *Journal of Marketing* 40.2, 1976, 17-24.

KAM-HON, Lee, Guang Yang, and John L Graham. "Tension and trust in international business negotiations: American executives negotiating with Chinese executives", *Journal of International Business Studies* 37.5, 2006, 623.

KOLB, D. A. *Experiential learning experience as a source of learning and development.* Upper Saddle River, NJ: Prentice Hall, 1984.

KOPELMAN S., and A. Rosette. "Cultural variation in response to strategic emotions in negotiations", *Group Decision and Negotiation* 17.1, 2008, 65-77.

KRAY, L., and M. Gelfand. "Relief versus regret: The effect of gender and negotiating norm ambiguity on reactions to having one's first offer accepted", *Social Cognition* 27.3, 2009, 418-436.

Latz, M. *Gaining the Edge.* New York: St. Martin's Press, 2004.

LEWICKI, R., Saunders, D. and Barry, B. *Negotiation.* 7th Edition. New York: McGraw Hill, 2015.

LEWICKI, R. J. *Trust and trust building: Beyond intractability.* Available at: http://www.beyondintractability.org/essay/trust_building (March 29, 2009).

_____ "Trust and distrust", *The negotiator's fieldbook: The desk reference for the experienced negotiator.* Edited by A. K. Schneider and C. Honeyman. Washington, DC: American Bar Association.

___, Barry, B, *et al. Essentials of negotiation.* McGraw Hill, 4th edition, 2007.

LIN Wusun (Translator), Sunzi. The art of war, Sun Bin: The art of war (Foreign Languages Press, Hunan People's Publishing House, 1st Edition, 1999)

LÓPEZ QUINTÁS. *El amor humano.* Madrid: Edibesa, 1992.

_____. *Descubrir la grandeza de la vida.* Estella, España: Verbo Divino, 2003.

_____. *Un nuevo pensamiento en la vida empresarial.* Estella, España: Verbo Divino, 2008.

LOWNEY, C. *El Liderazgo al Estilo de los Jesuitas*, Madrid: Editorial Norma, 2008.
LUFT, J. and H. Ingham. *The Johari window, a graphic model of interpersonal awareness. Proceedings of the western training laboratory in group development.* Los Angeles: UCLA, 1995.
MAALOUF, A. *Identidades Asesinas.* Madrid: Alianza Editorial, 2012
MALCA, Haydée Quiroz. "Un Granito De Sal. Su Circulación Y Consumo En La Costa Chica De Guerrero", *Nueva Antropología: Revista de Ciencias Sociales,* 22.70, 2009, 57-86.
MARDAK, Don. "The world of barter", *Strategic Finance* 84.1, 2002, 44-47.
MARTÍN Baena, E. "Pneumatología y Discernimiento Ignaciano". Madrid: Facultad Pontificia de Teología San Dámaso, 2003.
MATTHEWS, G. Deary, I. J. *Personality traits*, Cambridge, UK: Cambridge Univ. Press, 1998.
MENKEL-MEADOW, C and Wheeler, M. *What's fair, ethics for negotiators,* ed. Jossey-Bass, San Francisco, CA, 2004.
MESSNER, J. *Ética General Aplicada*, Madrid: Rialp, 1969.
MOSCATI, S. *The world of the Phoenicians*, transl. Alastair Hamilton, New York: Praeger, 1968.
O'HARA, M. "Relational empathy: Beyond modernist egocentricism to postmodern holistic contextualism", *Empathy reconsidered: New directions in psychotherapy*, edited by A. C. Bohart and L. S. Greenberg, Washington, DC: American Psychological Association, 1997.
OLEKALNS, M. and Smith, P. "Mutually dependent: Power, trust, affect and the use of deception in negotiation", *Journal of Business Ethics* 85.3, 2009, 347-365.
PATTON, B. "Negotiation", *Handbook of dispute resolution*, edited by M. L. Moffitt and R. C. Bordone, San Francisco: Jossey-Bass, 2005.
PEIPER, Josef. *Las virtudes fundamentales*, Madrid: Ediciones RIALP S.A., 2003.
PEREDA Bullrich, H. *La Salvación de la Historia*, Madrid: CPCR, 2010.
_____*Visión Bíblica, Ruta histórica de la Salvación.* Madrid: Fecom, 2010.

_____ *2000 años de Cristianismo, Historiograma del camino de la Iglesia*. Fecom, Madrid, 2008.

PEREZ-ACINNO, J. R. "Unamón revisado", *Intercambio y comercio preclásico en el Mediterráneo: I Coloquio del CEFYP*, Madrid: 2000, 1-7.

PIEPPER J. *Las Virtudes Fundamentales*, Madrid: Rialp, 1990.

PIETRONI D., G. Van Kleef and C. De Dreu. *Response modes in negotiation*, Group Decision and Negotiation 17.1, 2008, 31-49.

PRESTWICH, Roger. "Cross-cultural negotiating: A Japanese-American case study from higher education", *International Negotiation* 12.1, 2007, 29-55.

RABADAN Pérez, F. "Neofisiocracia, Método Aiio", *La Economia del Orden Natural y la Empresa Española*, Madrid, Junio 2015, Universidad CEU San Pablo.

RAIFFA, Howard. *The art & science of negotiation*, Cambridge, MA: Harvard University Press, 1982.

RIVERS, Cheryl and Anne Louise Lytle. "Lying, cheating foreigners!! Negotiation ethics across cultures", *International Negotiation* 12.1, 2007, 1-28.

ROBERGE. JF., and Lewicki, R. "Should we trust grand bazaar carpet sellers?" *Venturing Beyond the Classroom: Rethinking Negotiation Teaching Series, vol 2,* edited by Hamline Professor of Law James Coben, Hamline International Professor of ADR Law & Practice Giuseppe De Palo, and Christopher Honeyman, 2010.

SAINI, A and K. Martin. "Strategic risk-taking Propensity: The role of ethical climate and marketing output control", *Journal of Business Ethics* 90.4, 2009, 593.

SASS, B. "Wenamun and his Levant, 1075 B.C. or 925 B.C.?", *Egypt and the Levant*, 12, 2002, pp. 247-255. Disponible en: https://www.academia.edu/928041/2002._Sass_B._Wenamun_and_his_Levant_1075_B.C._or_925_B.C._Egypt_and_the_Levant_12_247_255

SCHELLING, T. *The strategy of conflict*, Cambridge: Harvard University Press, 1960.

SRIVASTAVA, Joydeep and Shweta Oza. "Effect of response time on perceptions of bargaining outcomes", *Journal of Consumer Research* 33.2, 2006, 266-272.

SMITH, H. C. *Sensitivity training: The scientific understanding of individuals*, New York: McGraw Hill, 1973.

SARTORI, Giovanni. *¿Qué es la democracia?*, México: Taurus, edición revisada, 2007.

SOSA, C. *Propuesta para un nuevo orden educativo, formativo y de capacitación profesional y laboral*. Buenos Aires, Argentina: Forthcoming, 2012.

SPAEMAN, R. *Crítica de las utopías políticas*, España: S.A. EUNSA Ediciones Universidad de Navarra, 1979.

STANTON, F. *Great negotiations: Agreements that changed the world*. Yardley, PA: Westholme Publishers, 2010.

STIEGLITZ, Robert R. *The geopolitics of the Phoenician littoral in the Early Iron Age, BASOR*, 1990, 297.

STRAUSS. *'Negotiations: Varieties, contexts, processes, and social order'*, Social and Behavioral Science Series, Jossey-Bass Inc Pub, 1978.

SWAAB R., M. Kern, D. Diermeier, and V. Medvec. "Who says what to whom? The impact of communication setting and channel on exclusion from multiparty negotiation agreements", *Social Cognition* 27.3, 2009, 385-401.

TADELE, Feleke. "Barter in practice: A case study of liwac transaction in Addis Ababa", *Development in Practice* 10.2, 2000, 223.

TAK, W.Y, and Hung, K. L. "How do personality traits affect construction dispute negotiation? Study of Big Five personality model", *Journal of Construction Engineering and Management* ©, ASCE (3), 2011, 168-179.

THOMAS D. and Inkson, K. *Cultural intelligence: People skills for global business*. BK Publishers, 2004.

THOMAS, K. W. and R. H. Kilmann. *Thomas-Kilmann Conflict Mode Instrument*, Tuxedo, NY: XICOM, Inc, 1974.

THOMPSON, L. *The mind and heart of the negotiator*. 6th Edition. New York: Pearson Publishing, 2014.

TINSLEY, C., S. Cheldelin, A. Schneider, and E. Amanatullah. "Women at the bargaining table: Pitfalls and prospects", *Negotiation Journal* 25.2, 2009, 233-248.

TRIVERS, R. L. "The evolution of reciprocal altruism", *Quarterly Review of Biology* 46(1), 1971, 35-57.

TVERSKY, A., and D. Kahneman. "The framing of decisions and

psychology of choice", *Science* 211, 1981, 453-458.
VELDEN, F., B. Beersma, and C. De Dreu. "Goal expectations meet regulatory focus: How appetitive and aversive competition influence negotiation", *Social Cognition* 27.3, 2009, 437-454.
VIDAL, J. "Violencia fenicia en el Mediterráneo Oriental", *Antiguo Oriente*, 6, 2008, 213-228.
WADE-BENZONI, K. "Giving future generations a voice." In *The negotiator's fieldbook: The desk reference for the experienced negotiator*, edited by A. K. Schneider and C. Honeyman, Washington, DC: American Bar Association, 2006.
WALTON and McKersie. *A behavioral theory of labor negotiations: An analysis of a social interaction system,* ILR Press books, 1965; Cornell University Press, 1991.
WATZLAWICK, P., J. Weakland, and R. Fisch, *Change: Principles of problem formation and problem resolution*, New York, 1971.
WIDELL, Magnus. "Some reflections on Babylonian exchange during the end of the Third Millennium BC", *Journal of the Economic & Social History of the Orient* 48.3, 2005, 388-400.
YIFENG, N., D. Tjosvold, and W. Peiguan. "Effects of warm-heartedness and reward distribution on negotiation", *Group Decision and Negotiation* 17.1, 2008, 79-96.
YOUNG, M. "Sharks, saints, and Samurai: The power of ethics in negotiations", *Negotiation Journal* 24.2, 2008, 145-155.
YOUNG, Oran R. "Politics of international regime formation: Managing natural resources and the environment", *International Organization*, 1989, 349-376.
ZANOTTI, G.J. *Economía de Mercado y Doctrina Social de la Iglesia*, Editorial de Belgrado, 1985.
ZARTMAN, I.W. and Berman, M. *The practical negotiator*, New Haven: Yale University Press, 1982.

Other resources:

http://www.orientalia.com.es/el-relato-de-wenamon/
http://phoenicia.org/wenamun.htm
http://patrimoniofenicio.blogspot.com.es/2009/01/el-relato-de-wenamon.html

Secrets of Archaeology: Sailing with the Phoenicians. (DVD 2003) Wheeling, IL: Film Ideas.

Contact: hchamoun@me.com